AF323207

# BUILDING FORWARD BETTER

**An Equitable, Sustainable, Inclusive Future for Asia and the Pacific**

# BUILDING FORWARD BETTER

## An Equitable, Sustainable, Inclusive Future for Asia and the Pacific

Bambang Susantono

Diponegoro University, Indonesia

NEW JERSEY • LONDON • SINGAPORE • BEIJING • SHANGHAI • TAIPEI • CHENNAI

*Published by*

World Scientific Publishing Co. Pte. Ltd.

5 Toh Tuck Link, Singapore 596224

*USA office:* 27 Warren Street, Suite 401-402, Hackensack, NJ 07601

*UK office:* 57 Shelton Street, Covent Garden, London WC2H 9HE

Library of Congress Control Number: 2025010547

**British Library Cataloguing-in-Publication Data**
A catalogue record for this book is available from the British Library.

**BUILDING FORWARD BETTER**
**An Equitable, Sustainable, Inclusive Future for Asia and the Pacific**



ISBN 978-981-98-1319-3 (hardcover)
ISBN 978-981-98-1320-9 (ebook for institutions)
ISBN 978-981-98-1321-6 (ebook for individuals)

For any available supplementary material, please visit
https://www.worldscientific.com/worldscibooks/10.1142/14314#t=suppl

Desk Editors: Selas Hamilton/Kura Sunaina

Typeset by Stallion Press
Email: enquiries@stallionpress.com

*To Lusie Indrawati who always lights up my day and
sparks up my soul*

# Foreword

The coronavirus disease 2019 (COVID-19) pandemic has left a lasting impact on history, exposing weaknesses in global systems while also providing a rare chance for introspection and transformation. The Asia–Pacific region faced immense challenges ranging from health crises to economic issues. Yet, in the wake of this adversity, the pandemic has also underscored the urgent need for new approaches to development. This book examines how the pandemic interrupted development progress, but more crucially, how future policies, financial strategies, and investments can drive the necessary changes to restore the region to a path of equitable, sustainable, and more inclusive growth and development. Rather than simply "building back better," we must strive to "build forward better."

In the chapters that follow, we explore a range of topics for this forward-looking approach. We begin by examining the accelerated digital transformation and the need for universal access, then explore the pandemic's impact on education and the importance of lifelong learning. The focus shifts to climate resiliency, climate finance, and the crucial role of infrastructure and connectivity in regional integration. Finally, we address strategies for advancing the Sustainable Development Goals, with particular attention to gender and youth. Through the lens of lessons learned from the pandemic, this book invites policymakers, leaders, and communities to embrace transformative solutions that will pave the way toward an Asia–Pacific region that thrives in the face of challenges and leads the global shift toward a fairer, more inclusive and sustainable future.

# About the Author

**Bambang Susantono** is a technocrat and distinguished development professional with over 30 years of experience in many national and international fora. He was a *Special Envoy to the President for the International Cooperation of the National Capital Development, Republic of Indonesia.* From 2022 to 2024, he was the *Chairman of the Nusantara National Capital Authority* of the Republic of Indonesia. Both positions are at a ministerial level, working directly under the President of the Republic of Indonesia.

Previously, Dr. Susantono was the Vice President of Knowledge Management and Sustainable Development of the Asian Development Bank (ADB) between 2015 and 2022. He was responsible for managing ADB's Sustainable Development and Climate Change Department,

Economic Research and Regional Cooperation Department, and External Relations Department.

Before ADB, Dr. Susantono was Indonesia's Vice Minister of Transportation and, prior to that, Deputy Minister for Infrastructure and Regional Development at the Coordinating Ministry of Economic Affairs. He chaired several research institutes, taught in universities, and was previously commissioner for airline, port, telco, and media companies.

Among other activities in international organizations, Dr. Susantono currently serves as a Special Advisor of the High-Level Experts and Leaders' Panel on Waters and Disasters, Special Advisor of the United Cities and Local Governments Asia Pacific, Member of Islamic Development Bank Institute's Board of Trustees, Member of Bloomberg New Economy Council for Cities, Member of Tech for Good Institute Advisory Board, and Member of Board of Trustees of Clean Air Asia.

Mr. Susantono holds a PhD in Infrastructure Planning and two master's degrees in Transportation Engineering, and City and Regional Planning from the University of California Berkeley. He got his bachelor's degree in civil engineering, specializing in Construction Management from the Institute of Technology, Bandung. He was also conferred an honorary professorship on livable and sustainable city from Diponegoro University, Semarang.

# Acknowledgments

I extend my deepest gratitude to those who contributed to the chapters of this book: Edimon Ginting, Guy Sacerdoti, and Sonoko Sunayama. Their insights and expertise have greatly enriched this work. I am also sincerely thankful to Pramesti Parameswari and Ekannisa Jasmine who worked endlessly to finalize the manuscript. Their dedication has been invaluable in bringing this book to completion.

My time at the Asian Development Bank provided me with countless learning opportunities, and I am deeply appreciative of the many individuals and studies that have shaped my understanding. Their contributions have been instrumental in my intellectual journey, and for that, I am profoundly grateful.

The pandemic has taught us a valuable lesson: Humanity must continually strive for a better future by creating safer, healthier, and more resilient societies. Let us build forward, better.

# Contents

# List of Figures

# 1

## Chapter

**Disruption and recovery accelerate
the region's transformation—
Build Forward Better**

People talked about "2020 hindsight" with relief. Then came 2021, followed by 2022. The challenge in dealing with the pandemic, however, was never hindsight. It was and remains foresight. And among the regions of the world, the Asia–Pacific region remains well prepared.

The COVID-19 pandemic started in Asia, and the region was first to feel its effects. It quickly spread worldwide and continued to evolve as new variants appeared, some more severe or contagious than others. At various stages, some governments imposed stricter measures than others. Regardless, the pandemic took a major human toll. Most Asian governments clamped down lockdowns quickly. That, of course, stymied economies, people's welfare, and mobility. Lockdowns and contact tracing slowed the spread of the raging SARS-Cov-2 (severe acute respiratory syndrome coronavirus 2) virus. But millions lost jobs. Tourism came to a standstill. Internal and overseas migrants couldn't move. Supply chains were disrupted across Asia.

Yet, despite the huge variations between regions, countries, and within economies, the Asia–Pacific region was able to begin thinking and planning for recovery relatively early.

Why?

Aside from 50 years of rapid—if uneven—development, most governments were able to provide relief and stimulus where needed. And the private sector, whether large or small, continued to innovate to stay afloat where firms could. For example, many economies were primed to take advantage of a digital transformation that was already in progress and which was accelerated by curtailed travel and personal contact. E-commerce surged to help satisfy demand. Supply chains and logistics adapted and grew. Financial systems embraced these changes and quickly upgraded the existing online banking infrastructure. Even small rural stores can now handle cash transfers and some online banking.

The pandemic may not be tamed. But with vaccines more available, COVID-19 is gradually becoming more endemic. Nonetheless, "new normal" continues to evolve. From a development standpoint, they must be "safe," "green," and more "inclusive." Investments must be more equitable and sustainable. The region's advantage is that most of these initiatives had started well before the pandemic struck. And that's why, even if somewhat surprisingly, many people from all walks of life understood that these are critical issues for Asia's future.

Technology will always advance, accelerating as new innovations grow popular. Data becomes more accurate. And it can be more easily shared. Managing all this new and complex information—whether asking people through face-to-face interviews or from satellite imagery of land use and climate change—has grown into both a formal academic discipline and a necessity for companies and institutions.

This book chronicles the speeches and opinions of Bambang Susantono. They describe how the pandemic disrupted development, but more importantly, how future policies, and finance and investment can accelerate the needed change and return the region to equitable, sustainable, and more inclusive growth and development. It is why we don't "build back better." We build *forward* better.

Why speeches? Oftentimes, prose can be tedious. Speeches, on the other hand, "talk" to the issues at hand. Here, they do two things. First, they identify the array of people from all walks of life who listen and are motivated by what is said. They address the more generic critical issues and describe what is happening in the Asia–Pacific within a regional or global context. The second reason is that speeches have a way of simplifying complex issues so a specific audience can easily understand. In addition, accompanying presentations amplify points being made, often via charts and graphs.

Aside from this introduction, there are seven chapters designed to cover the major issues that contribute to the region's ongoing transformation.

Chapter 2 describes the digital transformation that was already well underway when the COVID-19 pandemic struck, and how the process accelerated for individuals and businesses of all sizes, across all industries, and to some extent, across all countries in Asia and the Pacific. Universal access means no one should be left behind.

Chapter 3 discusses the impact of COVID-19 on education and skills development. The lockdowns during the pandemic disrupted lives, especially for school-age children and families, exacerbating challenges in virtual learning due to internet accessibility. The crisis accelerated the adoption of online education, underscoring the need for lifelong upskilling and reskilling to navigate digital transformations.

Chapter 4 delves into the increasing priority of addressing climate change in Asia and the Pacific over the past decades by building climate resiliency. Extreme weather events have become more frequent, prompting disaster preparedness measures in development agendas. The pandemic further emphasized the importance of reducing carbon emissions and preserving biodiversity, fostering international cooperation on climate-related issues.

Chapter 5 covers discussions on climate finance, ranging from carbon pricing, nature-positive investment initiatives, climate bank, to sustainable finance. Building climate resilience cannot be separated from the needs of climate finance. This chapter supports a similar climate change theme as Chapter 4, which is more focused on climate resilience.

Chapter 6 covers the topic of connectivity, from basic transportation and road safety to supply chain development. It discusses new ways to finance this more costly infrastructure—whether through land value capture or making green infrastructure more "bankable." It discusses infrastructure governance, and how expanding trade can drive better and more efficient connectivity.

Chapter 7 covers ways to better move toward achieving the SDG targets, especially those related to gender and youth. Mobilizing multilateral, public, and private financing to move the SDG process forward is a primary challenge.

The book concludes in Chapter 8 by discussing the main points of each chapter in support of the idea of building forward better.

# 2 Chapter

## Digitalization, the Expanding Digital Economy, and Digital Inclusion

## 2.1 Introduction

The digital transformation was already well underway in Asia and the Pacific when the COVID-19 pandemic struck. The crisis accelerated this process, both for individuals and for businesses of all sizes and across all industries. Digital technology holds the potential to boost global output, trade and commerce, and employment. A 20% increase in the size of the digital sector over five years (2021–2025) would increase global output by $4.3 trillion per year (or 5.4% of 2020 global gross domestic product [GDP]), while Asia would gain $1.7 trillion per year (or 6.1% above 2020 regional GDP) (ADB, 2021a). Global trade would rise by $2.4 trillion per year (5.5%) with Asia's trade up by $1 trillion per year (6.8%). The estimates show that about 140 million new jobs would be created per year—65 million in Asia (ADB, 2021a).

The problem is that all this growth is terribly uneven. There are huge discrepancies across countries and within countries in their digital transformation journey. Our job is to ensure that no one is left behind.

We must give people access to more affordable mobile and broadband services. E-commerce requires better logistics from value chain hubs to local communities. Yet the gap between the best- and worst-connected countries remains wide. Digitalizing customs and border procedures is important. So is access to safe and secure digital financial services. Training people in digital skills and literacy, particularly those working in small companies, providing access to information and communication technology (ICT) devices, and online teaching are critical. And regulatory systems must be established to protect personal data, prevent scams, and strengthen cybersecurity. Regional and international cooperation will help develop digital tax policies and effectively plug tax loopholes in the digital economy.

The sections here explain where we were as the pandemic struck, where we need to go, and what we need to watch out for on the way. They speak of the need for broader financial access through fintech, and most importantly, how to ensure "no one is left behind" in the ongoing digital transformation.

This following opinion written one year before the COVID-19 pandemic, was prescient indeed. In effect, it describes many of the changes brought on or accelerated by the health crisis. And it tells of the challenges many governments had already recognized and were preparing for when they needed to respond and act quickly.

## 2.2 Embracing Technological Advancements: A Path to Prosperity for Developing Asia

Technological advancements continuously disrupt our lives, offering new ways to conduct daily activities more efficiently and effectively. Traditionally, we rely on physical meetings at the office to interact with colleagues and clients. However, this trend is shifting as virtual reality emerges as an alternative for the workplace. Virtual reality offers benefits such as reduced travel time and costs, increased flexibility, and seamless collaboration across distances, enhancing productivity and work–life balance. This technology exemplifies how we can benefit from technological advancements with proper preparation for deployment.

We can see other examples of technology advancements and innovations on many others. Driverless cars, smart home devices, and robodelivery are a few of them.

We can't predict the future, but it's easy to envision an even greater proliferation of technology being a part of nearly every aspect of our lives.

The adoption of digital and online technologies offers significant potential for boosting the development of emerging economies, enabling them to leapfrog traditional stages of growth. Developing nations in Asia stand to gain substantially from this transformative period. However, realizing these benefits requires considerable effort from developing Asia, given the current lack of infrastructure for digital advancement. For instance, internet access remains limited to less than half of the population in the region, underscoring the need for improved ICT infrastructure to kickstart the digital revolution (GSMA, 2023).

A notable example showcasing the potential benefits of digital innovation is the Peshawar Sustainable Bus Rapid Transit Corridor Project in

Pakistan, aiming to enhance transportation services and air quality through the implementation of smart public transport systems (ADB, 2017a). Similarly, in Ulaanbaatar, Mongolia, the use of ICT in healthcare has eliminated the need for patients to travel to the provincial capital for medical treatment, streamlining medical record-keeping and improving healthcare access (ADB, 2021b).

Governments should leverage digital platforms to streamline public service delivery. For instance, in Suva, Fiji, there's a shift from paper-based land records to a blockchain-powered digital registry, highlighting the potential for transparent and efficient systems (ADB, 2023a). Similarly, global initiatives like Digital Thailand, Digital India, Taza Koom in the Kyrgyz Republic, and Digital Azerbaijan underscore the widespread push toward digital modernization. Nonetheless, addressing gaps in knowledge, experience, and capacity remains a pressing challenge for many developing nations.

The future implications of automation, robotics, and artificial intelligence on job availability are cause for concern, particularly for moderately skilled workers. Governments must proactively address these challenges by safeguarding workers and providing opportunities for skill development and retraining. By adequately preparing for the technological revolution, developing Asia can minimize risks and maximize benefits, ensuring a prosperous future for all.

This section discusses the progress made through digital innovation, just before the pandemic, and explores areas that could help policymakers navigate the challenges posed by digitization. As usual, private sector innovation sets the pace for a regulatory environment to catch up.

## 2.3 Unleashing Asia's Potential: Harnessing the Digital Wave for Financial Development

In today's fast-paced digital world, countries across Asia are witnessing a surge in online activity. Smartphones are everywhere. Many people shift to online platforms for shopping, banking, and other daily activities. However, governments are struggling to keep pace with this rapid technological advancement and adoption, finding it challenging to establish the necessary regulations for effective management.

The new "app economy" offers potential benefits, especially for developing countries. But to make the most of it while avoiding problems, smart policies are crucial. With more people getting internet access through smartphones, the way we do things is changing rapidly.

By 2018, over half of the world's population had gained internet connectivity, predominantly through smartphones, establishing them as the main conduit for accessing digital services (We Are Social, 2018). In Asia and the Pacific, mobile penetration rates reached 67% of the population, accounting for more than half of the world's mobile subscribers (GSMA, 2019).

This broad accessibility has catalyzed the expansion of the app economy, facilitating the dissemination of diverse content, goods, services, and entertainment. By 2018, India had achieved around 55% mobile subscriber penetration, fueled by the availability of cost-effective smartphones and wireless broadband services (GSMA, 2019). Similarly, smartphone ownership among Filipinos stood at 68% (GSMA, 2019).

The potential for digital innovations to revolutionize various sectors is vast, with significant implications for finance. Five key trends driving this digital transformation are intelligent systems, big data, cybersecurity, regulatory shifts, and digital workplaces. Furthermore, three notable innovations exemplify the potential changes within financial services (ADB, 2022a).

One such innovation is distributed ledger technology, most notably showcased through blockchain. Central banks in Japan, Thailand, Singapore, and Cambodia are actively researching or experimenting with wholesale digital currency applications using this technology.

Another transformative innovation is artificial intelligence (AI) and machine learning. These technologies are capable of automating repetitive tasks precisely and continuously improving user experiences without explicit programming. Simultaneously, the private sector is leveraging big data to forge new connections, streamline operations, and enhance customer service and value. For instance, leading banks in Singapore and Malaysia have seen success with customer-focused big data initiatives.

The third innovation is the open application programming interface (API), enabling seamless communication between different software systems. This integration empowers businesses, including those in finance, to efficiently and securely share functions and data with internal users and external parties.

However, cyber threats come as a threat to the rapid advancement of technology, particularly within financial services. Research indicates that cybercrime may have incurred global losses of $600 billion in 2017—nearly twice the amount lost to natural and human-made disasters (CSIS and McAfee, 2018). Governments, businesses, and individuals must stay vigilant, continually updating their cybersecurity strategies. Financial institutions are making strides in enhancing their defenses. But regulators and supervisors must also prioritize preventing the adverse impacts of cyberattacks on financial systems.

Governments in India, the Philippines, and Nepal are leveraging technologies to bolster their regulatory and supervisory functions, particularly within the financial sector. These technologies are called "regtech" and "suptech." Central banks also have regulatory sandboxes to explore innovative approaches and identify potential gaps. For instance, the Philippine Central Bank invited Cantilan Bank to participate in its sandbox initiative. The Cantilan Bank transitioned its core banking system to a cloud-based infrastructure (ADB, 2019a).

Furthermore, with increased task automation, the nature of available jobs will face significant changes. Investing in workforce upskilling is necessary to prepare individuals for future employment opportunities.

Policymakers in Asia should turn their attention to three key areas (ADB, 2022a). Firstly, there's a need for meticulous policy actions to mitigate risks and prevent unintended consequences. Prioritizing information security, data protection, consumer rights, and financial stability is crucial for a balance between fostering innovation and addressing associated risks.

Secondly, swift and innovative policy interventions are necessary to manage the potential economic and financial spillovers resulting from rapid digital advancement. Given the increasing interconnectedness of Asian financial markets with global counterparts, digital technologies have the potential to accelerate the spread of financial contagion. Leveraging existing forums like the ASEAN+3 finance process can facilitate regular policy discussions on fintech development and financial stability.

Finally, nations should adopt comprehensive digital strategies to guarantee broad accessibility and engagement in the digital marketplace. Establishing an environment where all individuals can derive value from digital innovations and lead secure and fruitful digital lifestyles is important. Ensuring no one is excluded from the opportunities presented by the digital age is paramount.

> The pandemic amplified the need to further digitize the finance sector. It has already expanded online banking and digital payment systems, highlighting fintech's potential to continue innovating and ensure business continuity. While fintech brings benefits, it also poses risks that regulators and policymakers must address to ensure innovation continuity, financial stability, and customer protection.

## 2.4 Navigating Fintech: Balancing Innovation and Regulation

More than 20 years ago, the world's first mobile money service was launched in the Philippines. This service was named Smart Money and was launched by Smart Communications in partnership with Banco de Oro (BDO) (GSMA, 2012). The service sought to fill a gap left by the limited reach of banking infrastructure in the country. At the time, few expected bank transactions would soon be carried out from the small smartphone devices that many carry today.

Over time, we have seen the rapid development of digital financial services from simple peer-to-peer money transfers to cutting-edge technology—such as crypto assets and distributed ledger technology, digital banking, and central bank digital currencies. Importantly, fintech gives us the opportunity to broaden financial inclusion. It offers increased financial access—and the delivery of new products and services—especially to the unbanked and underserved in rural areas. In 2019, investment in fintech across Asia and the Pacific from venture capital and private equity firms was a hefty $13 billion—and this in an industry that remains at a relatively early stage of development (ADB, 2022b).

Indeed, the COVID-19 pandemic underscores just how new technology can be quickly adopted and adapted to provide virtual ways of working.

The pandemic has amplified the need to further digitize the finance sector. It has already expanded online banking and digital payment systems—highlighting fintech's potential to continue innovating and ensure business continuity.

The pandemic has left the business world under major economic duress—and fintech is no exception. However, many are already rising to the challenge, adjusting products and services—and being creative—in meeting the needs of users struggling with the pandemic impact.

Fintech is already bringing significant benefits to consumers and investors, with new fintech solutions and evolving existing financial service providers. But the increased use of fintech solutions also carries risks (ADB, 2022a).

It is the regulators and policymakers that will be pivotal in balancing the promotion of innovation and invention, financial stability, and customer protection. This is essential for innovators, investors, and consumers to feel safe and build trust in an evolving environment, allowing the fintech industry to thrive and contribute to economic development.

To apply appropriate safeguards and mitigate risks, regulators and policymakers must understand, monitor, and supervise the fast-evolving, technology-driven developments that often come with new business models. Using appropriate tools and solutions—including new technologies such as regtech and suptech, used for managing regulatory processes and supporting supervision—will greatly help (ADB, 2022a).

Emerging technological innovations will be the heart and blood of fintech development—staying with us for years to come. If we think ahead when considering the existing regulations and policies, we can ensure their benefits will be enriched and sustained.

As we collectively work toward navigating this process, the continued support and engagement of each stakeholder is critical to developing responsible and inclusive digital financial services. We believe an inclusive fintech ecosystem is essential in supporting economic growth, greater equality, and reduced poverty during these challenging times.

> Digital solutions and financial technology, or fintech, are playing an increasingly important role in helping us cope with the COVID-19 pandemic and embark on a sustained and inclusive recovery. However, the pandemic has also thrown a spotlight on the stark inequality we face. Harnessing fintech for inclusive and sustainable development can pave the way for a strong post-pandemic recovery in Asia.

## 2.5 Leveraging Fintech for a Strong Post-COVID-19 Recovery in Asia

The year 2020 posed unprecedented challenges in so many ways. The COVID-19 pandemic quickly undermined development gains from recent decades and slowed down many Asian economies. Yet, every crisis presents opportunities. One would be the rapid advances in digital technology, offering a way forward for economic revival. In this section, I would like to discuss how we can leverage fintech development to foster the growth of the digital economy and pave the way for a strong post-pandemic recovery in Asia.

The COVID-19 pandemic accelerated the adoption and use of digital technology in many ways. The pervasive restrictions on mobility and lockdown measures drove more companies to shift their businesses and services online. The use of digital technology and e-commerce became the business norm, given the containment measures and consumer preferences for contactless transactions.

Digital payment platforms eased this transition from offline to online transactions—and their use in some cases skyrocketed. In the Philippines, for example, the leading mobile wallet company, GCash, reportedly saw a 700% year-to-year increase in transaction volume for May 2020 (ADB, 2021a). Its number of registered users also doubled during the first half of 2020. The public sector was also rapidly increasing its use of digital payments, which come in handy when delivering social assistance and related services during the pandemic.

Digital solutions and financial technology, or fintech, are playing an ever-more important role in helping us cope with the crisis and embark on a sustained and inclusive recovery. However, the pandemic has also awakened us to the stark inequality we face. The costs and benefits of the pandemic response have been unevenly felt within and across countries. It has exposed inequality in income, education, gender, and geographic location—some of which are worsened by the unequal access to digital technologies and services.

The digital economy is a major driving force for growth (Figure 2.1). Asia has seen rapid growth in the digital economy, especially in creating

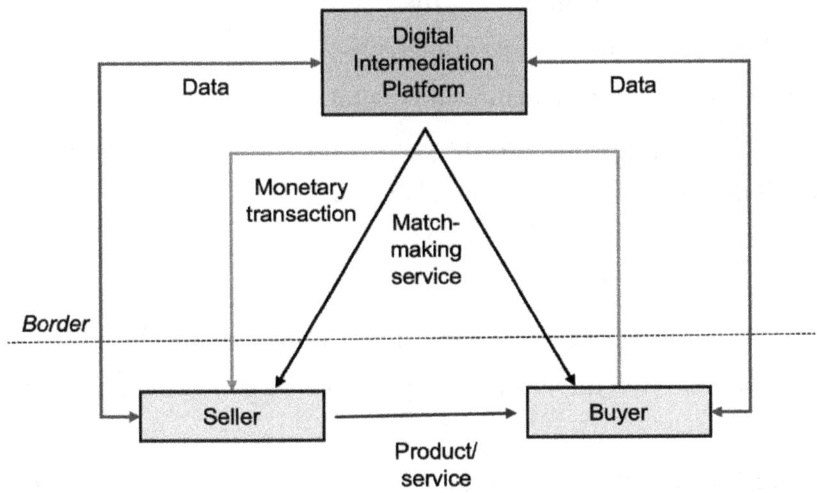


**Figure 2.1** Digital Economy as an Engine of Growth
Source: Adapted from OECD, WTO, and IMF (2020).

economic value through digital platforms. Asia accounted for around half of global retail e-commerce volume (Statista, 2024a).

New business models have proliferated with the rise of digital platforms, and they offer enormous economic opportunities. In 2019, digital platform revenues reached $3.8 trillion globally, equivalent to 4.4% of global GDP. Asia accounted for just under half of these revenues, while the United States constituted 22% of them and the Europe area 11% (ADB, 2021a). The use of digital financial services also increased consistently, with the rise in the use of digital platforms. The latest World Payments Report 2023 found Asia and the Pacific to be the global leader in noncash transactions, with $456.4 billion recorded in 2021 (Capgemini Research Institute, 2023). This number is projected to increase with a 19.8% compound annual growth rate for 2022–2027. The increase has been driven by growing smartphone use and e-commerce, and greater use of innovative payment methods such as digital wallets and QR codes.

These trends show that the digital economy holds great potential to reboot post-pandemic growth in the region. However, digital readiness across Asian economies varies considerably—and this includes the disparity in digital financial infrastructure and digital capability.

One of the preconditions for joining the digital economy is access. One billion adults in Asia lack access to formal financial services (World Bank, 2020). On the flipside, in 2022, 2.6 billion Asians had access to the internet, and 1.36 billion people were mobile internet users (GSMA, 2023; Statista, 2024b). Mobile and online applications for fintech services can draw in more of the underserved populations by providing access to the digital economy.

Policies that enhance fintech use can narrow inclusion gaps and boost economic activities. However, fintech also creates concerns such as data protection and cybersecurity. This means that policymakers need to balance the goal of fostering innovation and growth, with ensuring consumer protection and safeguarding financial stability. Let me discuss this more.

For fintech to help in an inclusive, more resilient, and sustainable regional recovery from the pandemic, we need to do five things (ADB, 2021a):

First, we need to ensure equitable access to digital and financial infrastructure.

Second, we must build an effective digital ecosystem.

Third, digital financial services must be anchored in the broader goal of inclusive growth.

Fourth, we can leverage fintech to catalyze sustainable development finance.

And finally, cybersecurity and safeguarding financial stability must be enhanced.

Let me briefly expand on each of these points, turning first to equitable access.

Asia continues to see uneven development of basic digital infrastructure and varying degrees of digital readiness. Economies differ widely, for instance, in their digital readiness. Steps should be taken to close the digital divide and expand investment in digital infrastructure. Providing digital education and training is also a key to unlocking the region's potential.

Second, governments need to develop an effective digital ecosystem to support the creation, diffusion, and scaling up of technology and innovation (Figure 2.2). The private sector will take on the major role of driving innovation. However, in most countries, public policy continues to play an important role in building the environment and institutions that are conducive to forging the critical links between financial and technology firms.

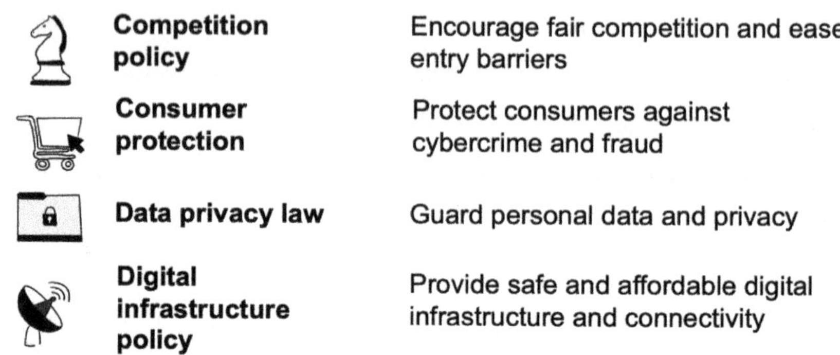



**Figure 2.2** Building a Digital Ecosystem (Develop a Complementary, Consistent, and Multifaceted Policy Ecosystem)
Source: Adapted from ADB (2021a).

Indeed, a complementary, consistent, and multifaceted policy framework is needed to develop and nurture a digital ecosystem. This includes focusing on (i) policy to encourage fair competition and ease entry barriers; (ii) consumer protection against cybercrime and fraud; (iii) data privacy laws that safeguard personal data; and (iv) a digital infrastructure policy that provides safe and affordable digital access.

Third, broader use of digital financial services can encourage inclusive growth and financial inclusion (Figure 2.3). Fintech applications through smartphone-enabled saving, crowdfunding, and security tokens could greatly enhance the efficiency of resource allocation and reduce transaction costs. One basic requirement for this is that measures improve digital and financial access. In developing Asia, the lack of a digital ID is often a critical stumbling block to all access to digital services.

In this context, a collaboration project between ADB, MiBank, and Women's Microbank in Papua New Guinea is a good example. The project focuses on a digital access tool to help low-income earners use financial services. Smart cards and near-field communication allow identity verification, even where there is no electricity or internet. This created greater business and livelihood opportunities. By eliminating some of the barriers

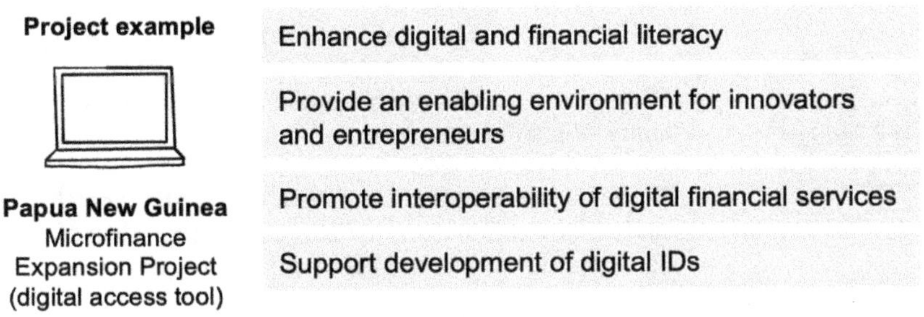

**Project example**



**Papua New Guinea**
Microfinance
Expansion Project
(digital access tool)

**Figure 2.3** Digital Financial Services for Inclusive Growth and Financial Inclusion
Source: Adapted from ADB (2021a).

**Figure 2.4** Fintech to Catalyze Sustainable Development Finance (Fintech Can Help Mobilize Finance)
Source: Adapted from ADB (2021a).

to identity verification and simplifying cumbersome processes for accessing financial services, this project has allowed many underserved people to tap into digitally enabled financial services.

Developing Asia needs as much as $1.7 trillion a year from 2016 through 2030 to meet its infrastructure investment needs (ADB, 2017b). This huge financing need includes renewable energy investment to meet low-carbon development goals.

This leads me to my fourth point (Figure 2.4). Fintech offers new ways to mobilize financial resources for sustainable development. For example, fintech platforms can be used to increase savings or channel resources into publicly or privately funded investments. They can also encourage the

**Figure 2.5** Enhance Cybersecurity and Financial Stability (Fintech Transforms the Financial Services Landscape, with Risks to Cybersecurity and Financial Stability)
Source: Adapted from ADB (2021a).

delivery of social goods and services and improve the efficiency of such service delivery. Blockchain-based solutions and asset tokenization also offer promising ways to close the substantial financing gaps and secure sustainable funding for infrastructure.

Advances in fintech and digital financial platforms have transformed "how" and "which" financial institutions deliver services. Yet, innovations also carry risks, and this is my fifth and last point (Figure 2.5).

As economies increasingly rely on digital finance, the disruption of a financial institution's digital operations has become more costly. Also, criminal activities to corrupt or destroy data integrity and privacy could become a heightened risk. So is the risk of fraudulent activities to divert funds elsewhere. Cyberattacks threaten financial stability, not only through direct costs on financial institutions but also the loss of confidence in financial systems and data integrity. One recent example was the 2016 attack on Bangladesh Bank, which robbed $81 million (Zetter, 2016). This damaged the bank's reputation and public trust, which are often fundamental to financial stability.

Financial institutions need a holistic approach to fortify their cyber defense and security. This can be done by reducing risks and strengthening the ability to recover quickly after an attack. They need to build platforms to share intelligence on incidents, including in real time. Governments also need to ensure their regulatory systems continuously adapt to the ever-evolving global digital landscape.

International cooperation is essential to ensure cybersecurity and financial stability—there are no borders in cyberspace or the digital world. Governments, central banks, regulators, and financial institutions must collaborate to build a safe global digital financial landscape.

Fintech advances also allow for better regulation of financial systems through applications of "regtech" and "suptech."

You are all familiar with the emergence of regtech after the global financial crisis. The technology allowed financial institutions to use big data, blockchain technology, biometrics, and cryptography to meet new compliance and reporting obligations. Regtech can deliver efficiency gains on multiple fronts, while boosting analytical capabilities and standardizing data management.

Suptech, on the other hand, offers efficiency gains by digitizing data, streamlining operations, and automating supervisors' reporting and data collection. It can help standardize reporting and regulatory practices, simplify data architecture among financial institutions, and handle the massive volume of new data as the digital economy grows. Real-time evaluation is increasingly needed, given the new sources of risk to systemic stability. It is also important in today's context, where increased financial interconnectedness can also heighten financial volatility.

Together, regtech and suptech add to the safety of financial systems in smarter, more efficient, and less costly ways.

Digital technology can be the lynchpin in Asia's economic recovery. Fintech has great potential to advance sustained economic development, financial inclusion, and stability. To realize its full benefits, policymakers must work together to leverage the gains from technology, while strong regional financial cooperation can help safeguard cybersecurity and financial stability.

The COVID-19 pandemic accelerated the adoption of digital technology such as e-payments and digital banking, and online retail sales in Asia and the Pacific. Post-pandemic economic recovery could greatly benefit from the enormous opportunities financial technology (fintech) offers for promoting inclusive and sustainable growth. For this, national policies, supported by public and private sector coordination, are vital. Regional cooperation also plays a crucial role in achieving the full potential of fintech and tackling its associated risks.

## 2.6 Fintech Revolution in Asia: Driving Inclusive Economic Growth Amidst Challenges

In the digital age, financial technology (fintech) solutions have emerged as indispensable tools, powering round-the-clock financial transactions and bolstering various sectors such as e-commerce and online banking. As the world grapples with the challenges posed by the COVID-19 pandemic, the role of fintech in fostering inclusive economic recovery in Asia has come into focus. Fintech solutions must reach marginalized groups, especially those in poverty and remote areas, both during the crisis and beyond. This section delves into the growth of fintech in the region, highlighting its transformative potential, challenges, and the need for collaborative action to harness its benefits effectively.

The COVID-19 outbreak underscored the vital role of digitalization in enabling secure and convenient financial transactions from a distance. With lockdowns and social distancing measures in place, consumers embraced digital platforms for shopping, banking, and conducting various economic transactions, thereby accelerating the growth of fintech. In the Philippines, the leading mobile wallet provider, GCash, experienced a remarkable 254% year-on-year surge in transaction volume in 2020, expanding its user base from 20 million in 2019 to 33 million in 2020 (Globe Telecom Inc, 2021).

However, the Asian fintech ecosystem had been rapidly expanding even before the pandemic, and this growth has continued since. Between 2016 and 2019, the number of fintech firms in the ASEAN (Association of Southeast Asian Nations) region focusing on digital payments, lending, and crowdfunding more than doubled. As many as 4,030 firms were using fintech in 2022 (UOB *et al.*, 2020, 2022). Additionally, the number of disclosed fintech funding deals nearly increased eightfold between 2016 and 2019, with Singapore leading the way. By 2022, these deals totaled $4.3 billion in funding (UOB *et al.*, 2020, 2022).

Fintech solutions in Asia and the Pacific concentrate on lending and payments, while the more mature, sophisticated segments focus on asset management, enterprise finance technology for financial institutions, and InsurTech (CCAF *et al.*, 2019). This information is from the studies conducted by the Cambridge Centre for Alternative Finance (CCAF), the Asian Development Bank Institute (ADBI), and FinTechSpace in 2019. In the last few years, payment systems have evolved profoundly as the ubiquity of mobile application payment tools, digital wallets, and QR code-based payment options attests. Figure 2.6 illustrates this trend, showcasing the growth of fintech firms and funding deals across selected ASEAN economies. Asian economies appear more open to adopting innovations like e-wallets than some advanced economies (de Sartiges *et al.*, 2020).

The increasing adoption of fintech is poised to drive further integration of payment systems, encompassing cross-border networks, ultimately leading to decreased transaction expenses (PayNet, 2017). In the year

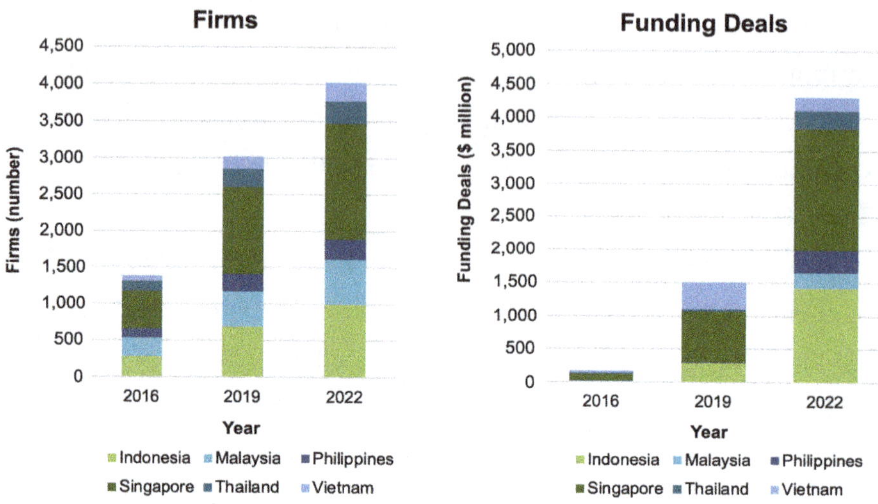



**Figure 2.6** Number of Fintech Firms and Funding Deals in Selected ASEAN Economies
Source: Adapted from UOB *et al.* (2020, 2022).

2019, the Society for Worldwide Interbank Financial Telecommunication emphasized the growing adoption of ISO 20022 standards across the Asia–Pacific financial services sector (SWIFT, 2019). These standards streamline electronic data transfer and messaging, amplifying the pace and effectiveness of data processing while fostering seamless interoperability among payment systems.

Driven by the imperative to modernize financial infrastructures, central banks across the region are actively pursuing the digitization of their countries' payment systems. A prime example of this effort is the visionary Bakong Project by the National Bank of Cambodia, which aims to revolutionize banking and payment services through an all-in-one mobile application. This innovative platform seamlessly integrates e-wallets, mobile payments, online banking, and financial applications, offering users a convenient and efficient banking experience compatible with any preferred bank account (Bakong, n.d.). Furthermore, the exploration of central bank digital currencies by several countries underscores the collective commitment to

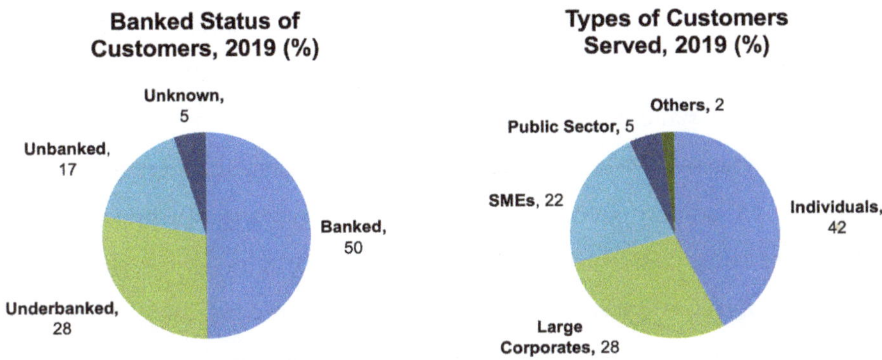


**Figure 2.7** Types and Banked Status of Fintech Customers in ASEAN, 2019 (%)
Notes: SMEs = small and medium-sized enterprises; 208 fintech firms that operate in the ASEAN region were analyzed in the study.
Source: Adapted from CCAF *et al.* (2019).

enhancing monetary efficiency and embracing the opportunities presented by digital finance.

Fintech holds significant potential in fostering more inclusive economic growth and financial systems across Asia and the Pacific region. Access to mainstream payment networks is vital in supporting individuals and businesses who are either unbanked or underbanked.

Studies carried out by CCAF, ADBI, and inTechSpace in 2019 confirm the importance of fintech in advancing financial inclusion, with 45% of survey participants reporting that their customer base includes individuals and businesses lacking adequate access to financial services. Of these customers, around 22% are small and medium-sized enterprises, slightly below the 28% represented by large corporations, with individuals comprising the remaining 42% (Figure 2.7).

The data from the Global System for Mobile Communications Association (GSMA) illustrates a significant surge in the total number of active mobile money accounts in East Asia and Pacific, increasing from 42.59 million in 2018 to 130.76 million in 2023 (GSMA, 2024).

This represents a threefold increase. Mobile money accounts can serve as an alternative for the unbanked by offering services such as deposits, transfers, and payments, especially in areas with limited banking access.

Lower transaction costs emerge as one of the key advantages of fintech solutions, particularly beneficial for migrant workers remitting money to their home countries. Research by Farooq, Naghavi, and Scharwatt in 2016 suggests that the cost of sending $200 using mobile money is approximately 2.7%, significantly lower than the 6% charged by global money transfer operators.

Fintech's advancement is reshaping the financial landscape, prompting a structural transformation across the sector. Digitalized banking services are gaining traction, driving down indirect transaction costs for consumers (Bachas *et al.*, 2018). Banks are expanding their digital footprint by embracing mobile applications alongside website-hosted services. Moreover, traditional financial institutions are turning to open banking initiatives to adapt to fintech innovations and overcome operational challenges.

Fintech is at the forefront of discussions surrounding central bank digital currencies (CBDCs) in Asia, with notable attention drawn to initiatives such as the pilot tests for the digital yuan conducted by the People's Bank of China (PBOC) (Zhang, 2021). These trials have sparked considerable interest and speculation within the financial community. Moreover, collaborative endeavors like the Multiple CBDC (mCBDC) Bridge project, which brings together multiple central banks and institutions, are dedicated to delving into the possibilities offered by distributed ledger technologies and CBDCs, particularly concerning cross-border payment systems (FSB, 2020). These concerted efforts signify a collective exploration of innovative solutions aimed at revolutionizing the future of digital finance and international transactions.

The emergence of digital banks is revolutionizing the banking sector across Asia, with governments across the region granting licenses to foster financial inclusivity and streamline banking operations. For instance, countries like South Korea and the Philippines have embraced this trend by authorizing digital bank licenses (Government of the Republic of Korea, 2021; Tonik, 2021). Notably, Singapore took a decisive stride toward establishing a digital-first banking environment with the approval of digital bank licenses in December 2020. However, amidst the proliferation of digital banking institutions, concerns arise regarding potential risks such as cyber threats and data breaches. These risks pose significant challenges to the stability and integrity of the financial system, necessitating robust cybersecurity measures and regulatory oversight to mitigate potential vulnerabilities.

To address these challenges, collaborative responses from governments, central banks, regulators, and financial institutions are imperative. Strengthening regional cooperation is essential for sharing information, harmonizing regulations, and intensifying investments and partnerships across borders. Addressing issues such as taxation, cybersecurity, and data localization requires coordinated efforts and a common multilateral framework to enhance the effectiveness of existing regulations and mitigate regulatory loopholes.

The pandemic has worsened existing inequalities, such as gender equality and access to education and training. These inequalities have been exacerbated by the significant digital divide—the uneven access to information technology. Therefore, it is crucial that we bring everyone together to narrow the digital divide and build greater digital inclusion.

## 2.7 Inclusive Recovery in Asia–Pacific Amidst the Digital Divide

The Asia–Pacific region has navigated unchartered territory as we have grappled with the COVID-19 pandemic and its many effects. The process of easing lockdowns met many challenges despite remaining questions on how our societies will recover.

But as we adjust to the realities of this evolving "new normal," one thing is clear. A return to "business as usual" is unimaginable in Asia and the Pacific—a region that was already off track to meet the SDGs, even before the pandemic struck.

The region's economies are at risk of further losing momentum on specific SDGs. For example, gender equality, as envisioned in SDG 5, has long been a major challenge, holding us back from realizing the full potential of the people (UNESCAP, 2024). Women's economic empowerment has lagged behind that of men, with women's participation lower in the labor force.

Our young people are also paying a heavy price as the pandemic disrupted education and training, with learning facilities closed. Extensive work has gone into providing e-learning solutions in most countries. But the pandemic has worsened existing inequalities in education nonetheless. These inequalities have been compounded by the large digital divide—the uneven access to information technology.

Given these realities, it is crucial to unite efforts in narrowing the digital divide and fostering greater inclusion. Tech companies play a pivotal role in this process, as they can both identify opportunities for positive change and address existing weaknesses that need to be fixed.

Enhancing universal access, improving all levels of digital skills, mitigating risks, and promoting open, inclusive, and ethical innovation are indeed cornerstones of any corporate strategy that fosters digital inclusion.

However, most tech companies still don't understand how crucial they are in shaping the digital future. I firmly believe they are the core solution to the inclusion puzzle.

The Asia and the Pacific region has made great strides in closing infrastructure gaps, upskilling its citizens, and, in the process building smarter, more livable, and interconnected cities. Yet, despite the vast majority of Asians with access to digital connectivity, billions still lack the ability to tap the digital economy, digital health, or digital education.

We clearly have work to do (ADB, 2022c). And we will not solve these challenges just by expanding network infrastructure or enhancing digital literacy—policy objectives we all must contribute to. It also requires access to affordable devices, tools, services, and content, accessible in local languages that offer real ways to improve lives and livelihoods.

The current pandemic has clearly shown that we all benefit from bridging the digital divide. We depend on bringing everyone on board if we are to successfully navigate and emerge from this crisis. It is crucial that we reach as many of citizens as possible, when providing public health advisories, tracing infections, and tracking essential supplies—whether food or vaccines.

As Asia and the Pacific economies adjust to the crisis and rapidly digitalize, entire market segments like tourism are put on hold. The informal economy that provides income to millions is disrupted. Yet powerful new businesses like e-commerce platforms are seeing rapid growth.

I am hopeful that increased awareness of digital inclusion among influential tech companies will help us generate new partnerships, promote ethical business practices, and spur action toward a more inclusive digital future.

As the world grows more digitally reliant, many governments are looking at digital transformation as the key engine to build forward better after the pandemic. The road ahead in expanding digital infrastructure will not be without challenges. Collaboration between governments, the private sector, and development partners is crucial for creating a prosperous, inclusive, resilient, and sustainable digital future for the region.

## 2.8 Utilizing Digital Infrastructure for Recovery and Growth

The COVID-19 pandemic has shown us the importance of digital connections in our daily lives. Amid the pandemic, maintaining physical distance from others to prevent the spread of the virus has become necessary. We have increasingly turned to online platforms as a primary means of communication and interaction. Hence, digital systems play a crucial role in helping us navigate through challenging times and facilitate our recovery and growth. As we move to "the new normal," it becomes evident that digitalization is not merely a temporary solution—it is fundamentally altering various aspects of our lives, including how we access healthcare, work, shop, and education. These changes are not fleeting; they are reshaping our future.

Governments recognize how digital transformation can help build forward better for a resilient and sustainable community. However, despite the accelerating pace of digitalization, Figure 2.8 illustrates that nearly half of the population in the Asia–Pacific region remains offline, posing significant challenges to social inclusion and economic progress, and deepening the digital divide (ITU, 2023).

The digital divide disproportionately affects marginalized groups, including low-income families, women, children, and rural communities, exacerbating the existing inequalities. Addressing this gap is imperative to

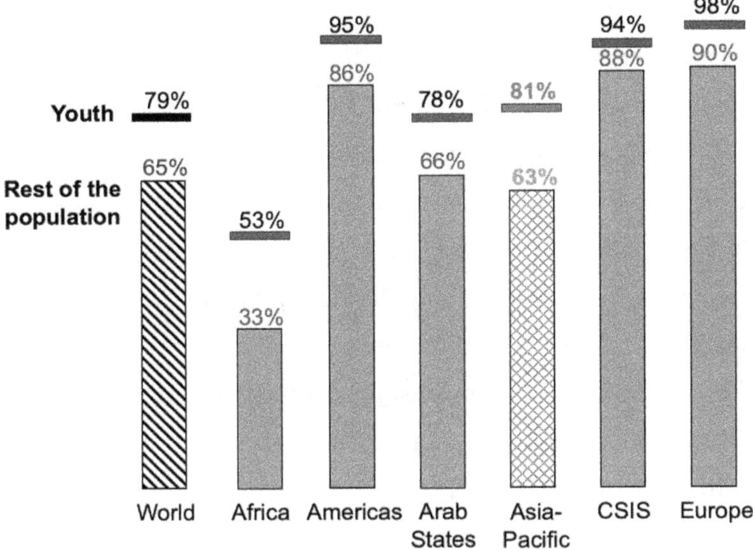


**Figure 2.8** Individuals Using the Internet, 2023 (%)
Note: Youth = 15–24 years old.
Source: Adapted from ITU (2023).

prevent the widening disparities and ensure that no one is left behind in the digital era.

To rebound effectively from the pandemic and ensure an inclusive recovery, we must significantly boost investments in digital infrastructure. The International Monetary Fund estimates that we need a significant global investment of $418 billion to bring connectivity to unconnected households through both public and private funding (IMF, 2023). This highlights the critical need for governments and development collaborators to prioritize digital infrastructure expansion as a strategic investment in the region's prospects.

Digital infrastructure extends beyond physical components, encompassing customized digital solutions to address the changing requirements of the public sector. For example, utilizing national digital IDs and digital payment systems has been crucial in broadening the reach of social protection initiatives to vulnerable communities in nations such as the Philippines and Pakistan (ADB, 2022c). Implementing cloud-first strategies within the public sector can enhance operational efficiency and flexibility in service provision, setting the stage for a more adaptive governance framework.

However, the endeavor to expand digital infrastructure is not without its obstacles. The swift progression of digital technologies demands adaptable strategies to foresee upcoming developments and implement creative solutions efficiently. Although the private sector has traditionally spearheaded digital investments, establishing a supportive policy framework is essential to promote continued private sector engagement in developing digital infrastructure (ADB, 2022c).

Finally, I want to emphasize the importance of seizing the amazing opportunity to expand digital infrastructure for a better future. A strong collaboration between governments, the private sector, and development partners is the key to prosperous, inclusive, resilient, and sustainable digital future.

# 3 Chapter

**Education
and
Skill Development**

## 3.1 Introduction

Pandemic lockdowns affect everyone. But school-age children were suddenly adrift. Studies, friends, and play were all out of their reach. Could they understand why? Had they done something wrong? When would life return to normal? Those in secondary school or in college or university understood, as many had the means to stay in touch. Those without internet were excluded.

Online education has remained one of the options for learning from the 2000s. But the pandemic made it a necessity. At the end of 2020, many countries had established online learning systems. But within and between them, there was stark inequality. For those without access, years were being lost. For those who were connected, entirely new teaching methods had to be learned and tested. For students, it was hard going. In 2021, some schools reopened, only to be shut down again as the COVID-19 infections resurged across the Asian region.

But accelerating digitalization and the increasing availability of online learning also made the necessity of future skill development more urgent. From trade apprenticeships to information technology, developing appropriate skills for the new or next normal is the only way to keep up with the changing trends. Lifelong learning is more than a catchphrase. It keeps people productive with earning potential far longer than they would otherwise.

The speeches and section in this chapter outline, and in some cases, detail just how critical education and skill development have become as the 21st century advances.

> The pandemic's impact continues to bring unprecedented challenges to all of us, affecting our health, livelihoods, and education. Critically, it exposed the widespread disparities in education and skill development globally, and more specifically across Asia and the Pacific. It threatens to reverse some of the hard-earned gains made over past decades.

## 3.2 Reimagining Education and Skill Development for a New (or Next) Normal

Tingting is a sixth grader in the People's Republic of China (PRC) who comes from a relatively well-to-do family. Through online open educational resources, she achieved ninth-grade level competency in Math during her one-year home-based learning. She also streamed Python* classes—an object-oriented programming language—and can now program simple games by herself.

In her comfortable home study space, she uses an iMac for livestream classes and open educational resources and an iPad and Apple Pencil for digital note-taking. She also wears an Apple watch that reminds her of her daily study and exercise routine. This is definitely high-end.

Linlin is a 36-year-old PRC tollbooth collector with 15 years of experience, who lost what she thought was a secure job. The pandemic accelerated service automation, replacing her with a radio frequency ID system. So, Linlin took a six-month online reskilling course in accounting and eventually found a new job.

What we are seeing is a widening digital gap—across age groups, countries, and regions within countries. We must fulfill the urgent need to equip students, teachers, and trainers with digital skills that allow them to adapt to new learning, training, and finding jobs in a rapidly digitalizing world.

Namitha is a third-year BA English student from India. To get a better internet signal, she stands on a tilted roof while attending online classes. Their roof is the only area in their house where she could get good connectivity.

This is too familiar in countries with poor information and communication technology (ICT) infrastructure and limited connectivity, especially in rural and remote areas.

Sharofat, a teacher in Uzbekistan, is also struggling with online teaching because of the same connectivity problem. She also lacked the digital skills to quickly learn how to manage her classes. Only from her roof could she use her phone to call and send messages to students. Still, she managed to successfully get all her students to the next grade level.

Even before the COVID-19 pandemic, research findings confirmed that a large proportion of children are not able to read a simple sentence by the end of grade 3 (World Bank, 2018). Globally, the learning crisis disproportionately affects the poorest countries where 7 out of 10 children are not learning basic primary-level skills. As early learning deficits worsen over time, students in disadvantaged backgrounds face severe long-term consequences in their adult lives. With a poor learning foundation, they enter the workforce as "educated" adults but ill-equipped to meet the skill requirements of the job market.

COVID-19 has exacerbated learning difficulties and inequities among the population since the overnight shift to online learning was not accessible to a large share of the population in many developing countries due to a lack of connectivity, digital content, and the readiness of teachers to manage online teaching. We must fulfill the urgent need to equip students, teachers, and trainers with digital skills that allow them to adapt to new learning, training, and finding jobs in a rapidly digitalizing world. Industry 4.0 has made significant impacts on the future of jobs, skills, and higher education. We have seen that the Fourth Industrial Revolution is likely to bring job displacements, job gains, and shortened lifespan of different occupations.

To address the compounded challenges, our education systems need to adopt a two-pronged strategy. First, it is important to go back to the basics to address the core problems of poor learning and skill mismatches, and related improvements required across all levels of education. Second, going beyond the basics, it is also important to pursue transformational approaches that include adopting education technology (EdTech) solutions to scale learning and equity, preparing the current and future workforce with Industry 4.0 skills, and improving teaching and learning by drawing on research from brain science, psychology, pedagogy, and technology. To capitalize on the emerging opportunities, let me focus on three key actions—convergence, cohesion, and collaboration (Figure 3.1) (ADB, 2022d).

*Convergence* comes from developments across disciplines, such as innovations in pedagogy, psychology, and neuroscience. Combined with technologies powered by artificial intelligence and big data analytics, education becomes a powerful enabler to transform learning and make it more equitable. Neurological breakthroughs, for example, show how the cultural environment alters children's brain development, which impacts learning

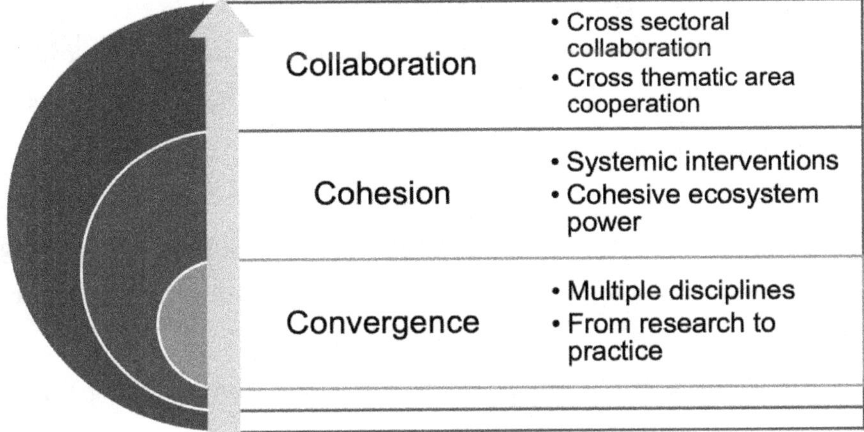


**Figure 3.1** Opportunities for Reimagining Education
Source: Adapted from ADB (2022d).

and school readiness. Discoveries in behavioral science show how early learning sets the foundation for success in school and life. These improve the lives of children and their learning experiences. The new understanding of neuroplasticity can help create new frameworks for adult education and lifelong learning.

A national survey from the National Center for Research in Policy and Practice in the United States found that the majority of education leaders value research and use it regularly (Penuel *et al.*, 2017). This convergence of research and practice can have a wide, more profound impact on schools, teachers, and students. Researchers and practitioners are now communicating more and collaborating with practice leaders. Education research—like research in medicine—can help shape the way school leaders approach their toughest problems and emerging needs. It can help leaders, managers, and teachers ensure children develop strong foundational skills so that as future skilled workers, technicians, or entrepreneurs, they can continually upgrade themselves—learning the new skills needed in the 21st century workplace.

Convergence impacts education and the world of work. In an interactive classroom, the teacher uses a smartphone to collect data for each student based on an individual card. She gets instant feedback from her students to more effectively manage her class.

Technology can be scaled up and empower personalized learning. Over the past 15 years, randomized evaluations have shown that teaching to the level of individual students consistently improves learning outcomes (J-PAL, 2022).

A student in Kenya has made great progress in math using Whizz Education's adaptive platform to address their individual learning needs. It is used by over a million students in the United Kingdom, the United States, and the Middle East (ADB, 2022d).

Arizona State University also uses adaptive learning with 65,000 students across 12 courses. Its Assessment and Learning in Knowledge Spaces was used in a college algebra course, increasing completion rates by over 20% for average students and 28% for those furthest behind (ADB, 2022d).

Tailored human support is important for integrating technology with education. Artificial intelligence (AI) and adaptive learning software can help students learn at their own pace, learn from their mistakes, and better understand knowledge. Teachers can use data generated by adaptive learning software to cater to each student, focusing on active learning and higher-order skills and combining cognitive and noncognitive skills.

A *cohesive* education ecosystem can scale up the capacity to integrate EdTech, to improve both teaching and learning. It packages the most effective innovations based on each country's situation, taking into account all the work done to build a cohesive short-, medium-, and long-term plan.

This ecosystem comprises five pillars—government policies, EdTech infrastructure, schools and teachers, students and parents (or caregivers), and those solution providers who together can transform education.

This ecosystem approach can systematically identify gaps and opportunities for improvement. For example, simply investing in devices—such as the one laptop per child approach without also improving connectivity and digital quality and training teachers will fail. It must be developed as a package.

Finally, there is *collaboration*. Education holds most importance in taking efforts to achieve all the Sustainable Development Goal targets. For example, a project-based approach focusing on science, technology, engineering, and mathematics (STEM) education can help students learn about issues like climate change, sustainable development, and entrepreneurial skills. It also helps nurture collaboration across priority sectors and themes to partner with a variety of stakeholders.

Let me conclude by posing three questions:

First, as part of rethinking and reimagining education for a new or next normal, how can new generation technology like adaptive learning help to scale up learning and increase equity and inclusion?

Second, given the blurring of post-secondary technical and vocational education and training (TVET) and higher education, how can TVET and universities collaborate with the private sector to improve employability skills?

And finally, how can artificial intelligence and big data analytics help develop a real-time labor market intelligence system that links emerging labor market needs with individual skill profiles for those seeking jobs or providing training?

The COVID-19 pandemic has underscored the importance of digital skills and competency. Tertiary education must adapt quickly to changes posed by Industry 4.0 and digital transformation to meet the demands of the new digital economy marketplace.

## 3.3 Digital Transformation in Tertiary Education in the Post-Pandemic Age

These are indeed troubled times.

In 2018, developing Asia stood to benefit immensely from a new era where digital technologies—including those millions of mobile apps—were vastly improving people's daily lives and transforming entire economies.

We knew even before then that the impacts of digital and online technologies would be massive—and transformational—with the potential to help emerging economies leapfrog development.

Fast-forward to today.

There was a time when we had to phone a restaurant for a takeaway. Now, all it takes is a few clicks and swipes on our mobile phone and our food arrives at our doorstep in an hour. Payment? All digital, of course. Nowadays, I hardly ever handle cash. I transact with a vendor on the other side of the planet using e-commerce, and logistics companies take care of the rest. My order is at my doorstep within days, sometimes even just a few hours.

This is now our "next normal."

The Fourth Industrial Revolution, or Industry 4.0, will significantly impact jobs, skills, and higher education. The job's lifespan, so to speak, will be shortened. And yes, Industry 4.0 will displace some old jobs. But it will replace them with new and more productive ones. Tasks will shift from routine and physical to those that require new, higher-order skills.

The time when graduates could sit on their laurels is long gone. Today, they need to commit to regular reskilling and upskilling. Lifetime learning will be the norm, and many will turn to tertiary education institutions to achieve this aim.

Tertiary education, therefore, must adapt quickly to these changes to help our next generation of graduates—and all other professionals—meet the demand of the new digital economy marketplace (ADB, 2022d). What we need is an agile and responsive system that offers targeted and well-designed "education and training on demand." Curriculums need constant upgrading, and digital technology must be both taught and used. In the longer run, this means that tertiary educational institutions must open up to students from much broader age groups.

Governments around the world recognize the importance of the ongoing digital transformation and also the elevated role to be played by AI and machine learning, as we go forward.

Several countries in the Asia–Pacific region are doing relatively well in embracing AI, according to the AI Readiness Index (Figure 3.2). The top-ranked Asia and Pacific countries are shown in the figure. However, Asian universities need to continue to do more to improve the quality of research and education and strengthen industry–academic cooperation. Their active exchanges with outstanding universities in advanced countries must also continue to grow.

It is clear that some tertiary systems are becoming strong leaders in expanding AI capabilities. In those universities, departments are moving away from their traditional silos to promote interdisciplinary approaches

| Rank (of 172 globally) | Country | Score | Rank (of 172 globally) | Country | Score |
|---|---|---|---|---|---|
| 2 | Singapore | 81.97 | 49 | New Zealand | 60.18 |
| 7 | Republic of Korea | 75.65 | 59 | Viet Nam | 54.48 |
| 9 | Japan | 75.08 | 65 | Philippines | 51.98 |
| 12 | Australia | 73.89 | 72 | Kazakhstan | 48.56 |
| 16 | People's Republic of China | 70.94 | 73 | Azerbaijan | 48.15 |
| 23 | Malaysia | 68.71 | 74 | Brunei Darussalam | 48.10 |
| 37 | Thailand | 63.03 | 79 | Nauru | 46.75 |
| 38 | Russian Federation | 62.92 | 82 | Bangladesh | 46.04 |
| 40 | India | 62.58 | 85 | Armenia | 45.22 |
| 42 | Indonesia | 61.03 | 87 | Uzbekistan | 43.79 |

**Figure 3.2** Government AI Readiness Index 2023 (Top 20 Asia and the Pacific)
Source: Adapted from Oxford Insights (2023).

that incorporate AI, data science, and data security technology. Several innovative university programs have begun reorganizing and converging departments. More institutions should pursue such innovation with the goal of developing high-quality talent pools.

Completing tertiary education substantially raises economic returns to education in general (ADB, 2022d). In particular, tertiary institutions can help scale up the students' opportunities for digital skills training, both offline and online. As mentioned earlier, in today's world of rapid digitalization, none of us can afford to be without a level of digital competency.

During the COVID-19 pandemic, the criticality of digital skills has been demonstrated in certain sectors that are central to dealing with the immediate effects of the pandemic—be they medical services or the care economy. It served as a reminder that the quality of tertiary education curriculum must be improved continuously to keep pace with changing workplace and societal needs.

Simply put, the pandemic transformed education. From online learning to the actual skills taught, it accelerated the shift toward teaching students how to prepare for a new, more digitized world.

## 3.4 Reimagining Education: The Role of Higher Education in Sustainable Development

The role of higher education in sustainable development cannot be more relevant as the global community faces unprecedented disruption from the COVID-19 pandemic. It reminds us that no matter how much we plan, there are times when our resilience is tested. From past lessons learned, we prepare ourselves for a volatile, uncertain, complex, and ambiguous (VUCA) world, as they say. So, it is critical for us not just to commit to sustainable development, but also to "walk our talk." This is where education in general and higher education in particular play a transformative role in ensuring sustainable development.

I will talk about three areas that affect our readiness to manage uncertainty and grow more resilient to ensure development is sustainable. First, the megatrends that affect us in multiple ways and set the global context in which we all coexist. Then there is education, which opens many doors that help us prepare for life and find the best, most viable ways to deal with emerging challenges. Then I will explore how higher education has influenced sustainable development—and will continue to play a catalytic role.

Let me highlight five of the most critical megatrends that affect our increasingly globalized world. First, almost all fields have been disrupted and are being transformed by technologies such as artificial intelligence, robotics, and automation. Aside from the rise of big tech, it is increasingly apparent in how we interact—be it social, through commerce and finance, communications, or transport, to name a few. One major debate is whether they will create more jobs than kill existing ones. The big challenges are cybersecurity, individual privacy, and universal access to a reliable, stable, and affordable internet. Overall, the potential looks enormous; no wonder Industry 4.0 has become the new lexicon.

Second, some countries or regions in the Asia and the Pacific will continue to grow with a large share of young people. South Asia is a prime example. And countries like the PRC, Sri Lanka, and Thailand are already aging (ADB, 2024a). They will require different approaches to service delivery and determine which sectors become priorities for investment and how they can still ensure sustainable growth.

Third, over 80% of growth is generated in urban centers (Sharif, 2023). Cities have become centers for innovation, a magnet for talent, and offer opportunities for sustainable and integrated development. These growth centers can generate and demonstrate integrated and innovative solutions by promoting university–industry linkages and entrepreneurship.

Fourth, the 21st century is being touted as the Asian century, given the region's continuing rise in share of global gross domestic product (GDP). If the region can maintain robust growth and avoid the middle-income trap, it will become the world's leading economic region by 2050 (ADB, 2011a). To sustain current growth, universities will need to play a greater role in capacity building and strengthening important institutions.

And fifth, with all the emerging opportunities for economic growth, we must remember the impact all these have on climate change—along with different shocks and disasters—like the one we are going through now. It is, therefore, more important than ever to commit to sustainable development. And in doing so, higher education plays a critical role in preparing people for leadership and equipping them with the technical, social, and political skills to manage the transition to a new normal.

When we examine emerging trends in education, we see how to harness new opportunities to strengthen the foundation of sustainable development. The biggest challenge is that, despite the remarkable progress in access and participation at all levels, improvements in learning have been slow. Wide skill mismatches persist despite expanding postsecondary enrollment. If students do not learn what they need to know, they will not expand their horizons, and their life choices will be limited. A significant number of people with low reading proficiency are noted to reside in Asia and the Pacific. In the region, 27 million children and adolescents are still illiterate, with 95% of them residing in South Asia (UNICEF, 2021). In many countries within the region, half of the children, despite completing their early grades, cannot read and comprehend a simple sentence by the age of 10 (UNICEF, 2021).

Additionally, beyond the quality of education, the relevance of the skills and competencies acquired is crucial for enhancing productivity and the competitiveness of individuals, companies, and nations. Education systems must better align with the demands of labor markets. Asia and the Pacific region face a higher average rate of skill mismatch (52%) compared to high-income countries (39%) (UNESCO, 2024). Undereducation is also a significant issue in the region, with 34% of workers possessing educational levels below the requirements of their occupations, compared to just 18% in high-income countries (UNESCO, 2024). This problem is especially common among informal workers.

Therefore, four emerging trends in education will help students become self-motivated, lifelong learners, and able to navigate the VUCA world much more effectively and practically (ADB, 2022d).

First, we need 21st century skills—those that include the 3Rs of reading, writing, and arithmetic—but go beyond to include digital and soft skills such as critical thinking, creativity, collaboration, and communication. Project- and inquiry-based teaching and learning that focuses on science, technology, engineering, arts, and mathematics—or STEAM education—produces risk-takers who learn from failure and develop entrepreneurial skills. The world needs cocreators, not mere consumers. And it is equally important to find exciting new opportunities for girls and women.

Second, new-generation education technologies powered by artificial intelligence and big data analytics will transform teaching through personalized and self-paced learning. Every learner is different and motivated differently. Adaptive learning technologies allow each student to master competencies at their own pace, while teachers monitor progress in real time and provide targeted support. This helps scale learning and equity.

Third, unlike in the past, students do not have to finish their studies all at once. Perhaps it is still necessary to complete school education. But beyond that, it is possible to concurrently learn and earn. With micro-credentialing, learners can stack different courses to get the best certifications for their chosen occupation, and best aligned with emerging labor market needs. This is why reskilling and upskilling is becoming one of the largest global industries—in collaboration with education providers and employers.

Fourth, as Sustainable Development Goal (SDG) 4 says, education quality is more critical than quantity. The learning crisis many developing countries face is about poor learning despite more education. Recent research consistently shows that rapid economic growth in Asia is linked to the quality of education provided.

Higher education of course plays an important role in sustainable development. Four areas stand out (ADB, 2022d).

First, for any developing country to move up the value chain, more highly skilled people are needed in research, development, innovation, and leadership, among others. Giving teachers and students the knowledge and skills to understand and support the SDGs should be standard practice in universities.

Second, universities can promote entrepreneurship and innovation skills to help address real world challenges, such as renewable energy, sustainable transport, and sustainable agriculture.

Third, universities are increasingly moving toward cross-sectoral collaboration using multidisciplinary approaches, such as land management and planning, and communication networks.

And fourth, universities are a reliable source for capacity building. But, as the current pandemic demonstrates, they are grossly underutilized and ill-prepared in many developing countries. With high levels of research and development (R&D) and cross-sectoral collaboration, universities in developing countries should build global partnerships to offer new ideas, disseminate new technologies, and collaborate across sectors, public–private stakeholders, and regions. They can develop and support the leadership needed to strengthen public engagement, initiate cross-sectoral dialogue and action, design policies, advocate sustainable measures, and show commitment.

As noted earlier, universities help prepare the expertise and leadership needed to advance different SDGs—such as poverty (SDG 1); health (SDG 3); gender (SDG 3); decent work and economic growth (SDG 8); industry, innovation, and infrastructure (SDG 9); responsible consumption and production (SDG 12); climate change (SDG 13); along with peace, justice, and strong institutions (SDG 16).

The important role of higher education in sustainable development is critical and undisputed. However, while enrollment rates in higher education have increased significantly in some countries, others are still experiencing slow growth. Gross enrollment ratios vary widely, ranging from less than 20% in Cambodia and the Lao People's Democratic Republic to over 50% in China, Kazakhstan, Mongolia, and the Republic of Korea (UNESCO Institute for Statistics, 2024). East Asia and the Pacific region witnessed the highest increase in gross enrollment from 2010 to 2022, with particularly rapid growth during this period (Figure 3.3).

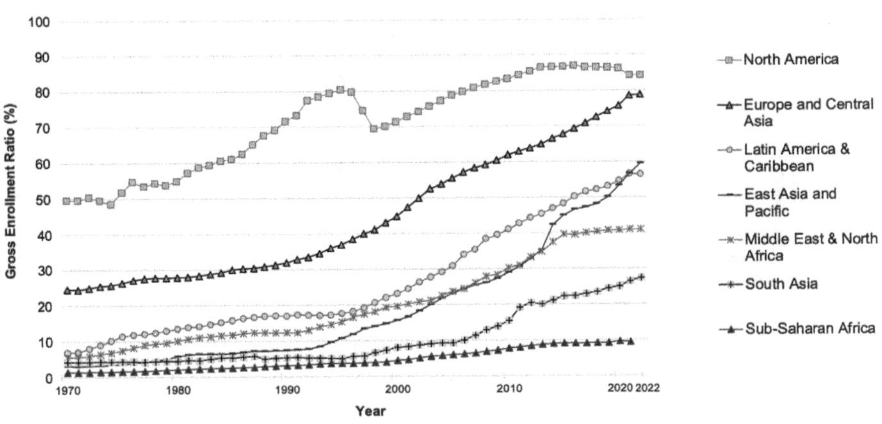


**Figure 3.3** Gross Enrollment Ratio in Tertiary Education, 1970–2022
Source: Adapted from UNESCO Institute for Statistics (2024), processed by Our World in Data.

Similarly, female participation in tertiary education also grew significantly with similar variations across countries. But gender parity remains a big concern in several South Asian countries. Some recent reports highlight the critical importance of optimizing women's potential in driving social and economic growth. For example, in 2018, a McKinsey Global Institute report, *The Power of Parity: Advancing Women's Equality in Asia Pacific*, estimated that improved gender equality in the region could add $4.5 trillion to collective GDP annually in 2025 (Woetzel *et al.*, 2018). So it is not only important to put more women in higher education but to help their transition into work and entrepreneurship. Countries such as Sri Lanka have high female enrollment in higher education; but their participation in the workforce is low (Figure 3.4).

In a world disrupted by COVID-19, it is important to reimagine higher education as it promotes quality, relevance, and equity. We see four inter-related developments (ADB, 2022d). First, while there was a gradual shift

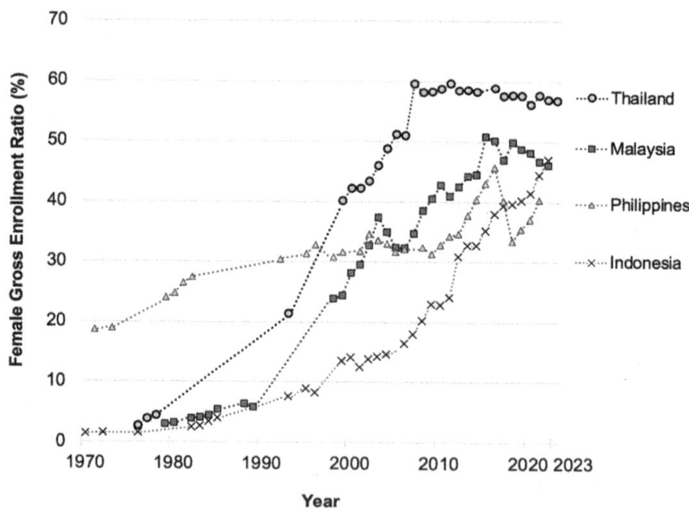


**Figure 3.4** Female Gross Enrollment Ratios for Tertiary Education in Asia, Selected Countries, 1970–2023
Source: Adapted from World Bank (2024a).

to blended learning prior to COVID-19, the pace has accelerated because of the pandemic. This helps meet the demand to make higher education more accessible and affordable without compromising quality. For instance, Indonesia is expanding access to higher education by allowing students to take up to 50% of their courses online.

Second, many countries are concerned about the lack of employability of higher education graduates, despite large public and private investments. In response, a new higher education model is evolving, driven by competency-based skills linked to employability. This shifts away from the traditional prestige-based models such as Harvard, Massachusetts Institute of Technology (MIT), and Stanford. Graduates in the Republic of Korea and, more recently, the PRC, already face higher unemployment rates. This forces universities to become more practical by forging employer partnerships for internships and apprenticeships. As a result, there is a blurring between polytechnics and universities, as their approaches converge.

Third, students can choose not to complete their four-year program in one go; rather, they take modular courses that stack up to degrees, diplomas, or certificates. Google already has a six-month technology-oriented program they accept in lieu of a four-year program. Micro-credentialing is already gaining traction. This allows students to learn while they earn. Singapore's SkillsFuture program is another example. The government provides vouchers to workers to upskill and reskill—keeping up with rapid occupational changes due to technological disruptions.

Fourth, as I noted earlier, universities are increasingly expected to provide integrated solutions to real-world problems. The current pandemic is a wake-up call that reminds us to do more to find integrated solutions for sustainable development. Discussions on the future of higher education should turn this crisis into an opportunity. We should all join the global effort to reimagine tertiary and higher education to speed the way toward attaining the SDGs. Promoting public–private partnerships can help address poverty, human capital, gender, urban development, climate change, and sustainable growth.

To conclude, higher education institutions not only prepare experts, leaders, and thinkers. They provide capacity development to other institutions, which together form an ecosystem for a post-pandemic transformation.

> The pandemic has upended even the best-laid plans despite many seeing it coming. Our development arsenal must include the tools of future thinking and foresight. Future literacy significantly improves the capacity of people to understand their fears and hopes, better comprehend global changes, create their own images of the future, and discover new possibilities for innovation and resilience.

## 3.5 Empowerment through Futures Literacy

We live in an increasingly VUCA world. The COVID-19 pandemic has upended even the best-laid plans. The pandemic is not really a black swan. Many saw it coming. It is actually a symptom of other problems and can be explained in many ways, with each explanation creating different solutions.

Clearly, our development arsenal must include the tools of future thinking and foresight: these include emerging issues analysis, scenario planning with radical change scenarios, and backcasting.

In 2019 and the beginning of 2020, stakeholders collaborated with the Asian Development Bank (ADB) in workshops focusing on future thinking and foresight. The aim was to enhance strategic planning and enable participants to shape the futures they envision for themselves and their communities. These workshops also aimed to assist leaders in contemplating the potential global, regional, and national challenges their countries could encounter in the coming decade. Below are some takeaways from the workshops:

- In Armenia, participants called for radical change, having joined the recent "velvet revolution" that changed its government.
- In Cambodia, participants imagined women garment workers turning into national leaders.
- In the PRC, they wanted to "unleash" knowledge and give it "wings."
- In Mongolia, they stressed that development partners must cooperate; and they highlighted the need for a common vision so citizens can hold politicians accountable, particularly since they often change.
- In Kazakhstan, participants looked beyond the dominant oil industry to artificial intelligence technology to enrich their country in the future. They examined how tourism would need to change if climate disruption continued.
- In the Philippines, they envisioned a less hierarchical economic planning agency.
- And in Timor-Leste, government officials, including those at the highest level, expressed a profound interest in the tools that might help them rebuild dilapidated infrastructure.

All these stakeholders saw that they could turn the future from a liability, a source of never-ending disappointment in false expectations, into an asset for seeing and creating a rich, emergent, novelty-filled world around them.

To navigate our volatile, uncertain, complex, and ambiguous world, people must become self-directed lifelong learners with 21st century skills (ADB, 2022d). They must learn the basics—reading, writing, arithmetic— plus digital literacy, soft skills, and occupational and entrepreneurial skills.

Education must not only prepare students for jobs but also turn them into risk-takers. We learn from failures to become more resilient. Students must become global citizens who value diversity, tolerance, and respect for each other.

As the biggest enabler, education must promote collaboration across sectors to achieve all 17 Sustainable Development Goals.

Traditional education will not get the job done. Only futures literacy can prepare learners to become cocreators who can innovate and sustain human-centric development.

> Education holds immense potential in addressing the climate crisis, yet its role remains under-tapped. Transforming education to instill universal values, promote sustainability, and produce experts in climate-related fields is critical for building a resilient future and mitigating the climate crisis.

## 3.6 Education as a Tool to Address Climate Emergency

Climate change is one of the biggest challenges to humanity, threatening ecosystems, economies, and livelihoods worldwide. With the impending renewal of commitments to combat this crisis at the 2021 United Nations Climate Change Conference (COP26), the spotlight is placed again on the urgent need for more effective solutions. While measures such as carbon neutrality pledges and policy reforms have gained traction, one crucial yet often overlooked aspect remains. Education's transformative role in climate mitigation and adaptation should become one of our focuses.

Education stands as a beacon of hope amidst the tumult of environmental degradation, offering a gateway to sustainable solutions and informed action. As world leaders grapple with the complexities of climate action, integrating climate literacy into educational curricula emerges as a cornerstone of long-term resilience and adaptation strategies.

In Asia and the Pacific, more than half of the global population resides, thus emitting significant greenhouse gases. The need for climate education is pressing in this region. In the areas where rising sea levels threaten coastal towns and extreme weather disrupts livelihoods, the impacts of climate change are more felt. Here, education becomes a powerful tool, helping communities face these challenges against the effects of climate change.

Education holds immense power to bring changes across various aspects, particularly in shaping a generation aware of climate issues (ADB, 2022d). By integrating values of global citizenship and sustainable development into educational systems, students can grasp the complexities of environmental challenges and their ties to broader social issues. Many schools are currently adopting sustainability principles. For instance, schools are organizing eco-friendly campus projects and community-driven sustainability endeavors.

Secondly, investment in inclusive education is paramount for building resilience against climate impacts, particularly among vulnerable populations. In countries like Bangladesh and Vietnam, where climate change exacerbates existing inequalities, targeted educational interventions are instrumental in empowering marginalized groups, including women and indigenous communities. By prioritizing access to quality education, countries can bridge socioeconomic disparities and foster collective action in the face of climate adversity.

Thirdly, education serves as a crucible for innovation and skills development, equipping future leaders with the tools to navigate complex environmental challenges. Whether it's advancements in renewable energy, sustainable agricultural practices, or waste management solutions, schools are pivotal in fostering innovative thinking and practical problem-solving. For example, various educational initiatives promote environmental entrepreneurship, encouraging students to develop sustainable business models that address pressing environmental issues. Moreover, collaboration between academia and industry further enhances the development and implementation of cutting-edge environmental solutions. Through hands-on projects and research collaborations, students gain practical experience and contribute to real-world environmental conservation efforts.

Collaboration between governments, educational institutions, civil society, and the private sector is indispensable in realizing the full potential of climate education. By forging partnerships and sharing best practices, stakeholders can amplify the impact of educational initiatives and drive systemic change at scale. Platforms like the Global Education Coalition for Climate Action (GECCA) facilitate knowledge-sharing and collaboration among diverse stakeholders, fostering a collaborative approach to climate education.

We're at a crucial moment, and changing education is super important. If we use education right, we can train a new generation to fight climate change. By working together and staying committed, we can create a future where education helps us protect the environment and stick together. This means teaching people about environmental issues and showing them how to make a difference. By doing this, we can build a society that cares about the planet and is ready to tackle big challenges.

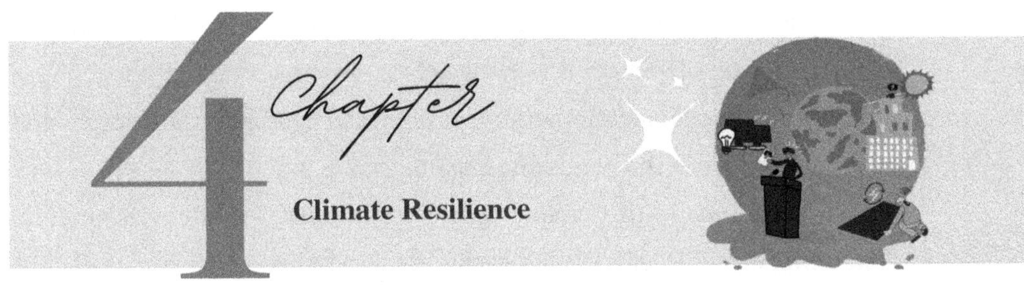


## 4.1 Introduction

Climate change mitigation and adaptation has grown as a development priority over 30 years. As extreme weather events intensified and associated disasters became more frequent, increasing attention has been given to building resilience against disasters—whether from flooding, coastal surges, wind, or landslides. Finding nature-based solutions and preserving or replenishing biodiversity on land and in the oceans has gained increased momentum over the past decade.

The pandemic has only accelerated these concerns. The clear skies over major polluted cities during lockdowns provided the public with dramatic evidence of what reducing carbon emissions can actually do. It also made clear to policymakers and development strategists that climate change and nature-based solutions have to become a major priority and an integral part of any post-pandemic recovery plan.

In fact, although it began prior to COVID-19, the pandemic acted to combine concerns over climate change, the environment, and resiliency. This convergence has gained momentum among international organizations and governments since the pandemic began.

The sections in this chapter cover the wide range of environmental issues that must be dealt with as we build forward better. Climate resilience is a major theme throughout, whether discussing nature's vital roles, air and water pollution, or community resilience.

This section speaks about the interaction between the COVID-19 pandemic, climate change, and the urgent need for nature conservation. It underscores the significance of the Kunming Declaration of COP15, which highlights the importance of ecosystems. Furthermore, this section also discusses the importance of aligning climate and nature agendas to achieve global net zero and protect biodiversity.

## 4.2  After COP15, a New Hope for Nature

The COVID-19 pandemic and resulting disruptions to the global economy—plus a trail of climate-change-related disasters—have thrown into sharp relief some longstanding weaknesses in key systems that affect us all: health care, global food production and supply chains, water administration, financial management, governance, and disaster preparedness.

But the most vital system of all—the one on which all others depend—is, of course, nature. All human activity is embedded in the world's ecosystems. Our health and livelihoods, indeed our survival, are all contingent on supplies of oxygen, food, and water. Our prosperity relies on natural capital, which financial systems are only now realizing is a measure of wealth as important as gross domestic product (GDP).

This new appreciation of nature springs from a bleak realization: we are rapidly reaching a point of no return in the decline of biodiversity and ecosystems. This is a result of the accelerated degradation of natural assets by human activity. Like all other systems, nature has also had to bear the ever-mounting negative impacts of climate change.

It is of paramount importance that we conserve the healthy ecosystems we still have and revive and expand those on the verge of annihilation—this is no less important than drastically curbing GHG emissions.

And so, the Kunming Declaration coming out of the 15th Conference of the Parties of the UN Convention on Biological Diversity, or COP15, is encouraging. More than 100 countries have signed the declaration, which aims to narrow the action gap between climate and nature conservation and financing. It agrees to urgent and integrated action to insert biodiversity into all parts of the global economy. It also announced a commitment for countries to protect 30% of their land and sea areas through effective conservation measures by 2030, increase the application of ecosystem-based approaches to address biodiversity loss, and strengthen legal and regulatory frameworks (CBD, 2022).

This momentum is important to further the nature agenda at the upcoming conferences. Nature loss is contributing to climate change, and climate change is a key driver of nature loss (Chetan-Welsh and Hendry, 2022). Mainstreaming nature with climate actions should be the new precedence. Multilateral development banks (MDBs) can help strengthen mainstreaming nature into investments and operations through technical support, analysis, and assessments that increase awareness and understanding of the role and value of nature in sustainable development (ADB, 2019b;

Larsen and Laxton, 2024; Nedopil *et al.*, 2024). It is now well recognized among all parties that there is no pathway to achieving 1.5 degrees or climate-resilient development that does not consider nature.

The consensus that crystallized among the MDBs toward the recovery from the COVID-19 pandemic is clear: the recovery needs to be oriented toward nature, inclusivity, and enhanced global resilience in the face of climate change and potential crises in human health and well-being.

Therefore, intensified dialogue and strategic collaboration among MDBs are required and not only among ministries of finance and implementation partners, but with the full range of partners: diverse public and private financial institutions, science and research bodies, and civil society.

Stakeholders have increasingly narrowed their common goals to focus on the following: securing global net zero by mid-century and keeping 1.5 degrees within reach, protecting communities and natural habitats—and mobilizing finance to sustain these efforts. But to make headway on achieving these goals, much depends on assigning the world's natural assets their true value—with ever-increasing precision; with universal recognition that nature is at the nexus of global survival, well-being, and prosperity; and with strengthened solidarity among policymakers and stakeholders.

One of the key achievements of COP26 is the finalization of the Paris Agreement rulebook. Achieving the goals of the Paris Agreement requires addressing not only carbon dioxide emissions but also other pollutants like methane and black carbon. While governments in Asia have initiated environmental policies and air quality action plans, additional efforts are needed to build forward better.

## 4.3 Improving Air Quality—Enhancing Local Cooperation to Address Worldwide Climate Issues

To achieve the goals of the Paris Agreement, reducing carbon dioxide emissions alone is not enough. Other emissions and air pollutants also matter, such as methane, black carbon, and ground-level ozone (WHO, 2018).

In turn, addressing climate change is beneficial for air quality. This is evident from climate change-related disasters, such as forest fires, that exacerbate air pollution through the emission of large quantities of particulate matter.

No corner of the world is safe from the devastating consequences of climate change. Around 60% of the global population and one-third of the globe's land surface area is in Asia (Boudreau *et al.*, 2023). It is home to countries that are most vulnerable to climate change and also accounts for over 50% of global GHG emissions (Marriott and Aggarwal, 2023). Thus, Asia's climate actions will determine whether the battle against climate change will be won or lost.

Asia also suffers from severe air pollution. According to Regan (2024), 99 of the world's 100 most polluted cities in 2023 were found in Asia, with 83 of them being in India. A staggering 99% of cities in South Asia and Southeast Asia exceed the World Health Organization air quality guidelines (Firdaus *et al.*, 2023; IQAir, 2018).

Air pollution has had significant negative health and economic impacts on people. A 2019 study showed that 20% of deaths in Bangladesh are caused by air pollution (World Bank, 2023a). Around two million premature deaths across South Asia were attributable to air pollution, resulting in significant economic costs (World Bank, 2023a).

Many governments in developing Asia are increasingly aware of the urgency to take action, and they are beginning to issue new environmental policies and air quality action plans in recent years. These include the Bangladesh Clean Air Act, India's National Clean Air Program, and the National Electric Vehicles Policy in Pakistan (World Bank, 2023a).

These national policies, action plans, as well as the support from development partners, will be important contributions to slowing climate change. But they are certainly not enough, and much more needs to be done before Asian cities improve their air quality.

At the COP26, several important pledges and commitments were made by the United Nations Framework Convention on Climate Change (UNFCCC) parties. Notable pledges from Asia include India's commitment to become carbon neutral by 2070 (BBC, 2021). In September 2020, the PRC also announced that carbon emissions will hit a peak by 2030 and the country will become carbon neutral by 2060 (McGrath, 2020). When these two Asian countries together are responsible for over 33% of global greenhouse gas emissions, we can say that how we will implement these climate commitments will make history.

However, despite all these pledges and commitments, the world is still headed toward a 2.5–2.9 degree increase in temperature, instead of the 1.5 degree target (UNEP, 2023). This means we have to take actions beyond the official commitments or else, we will not be able to save the planet. Reducing air pollution is an important part of the actions we need to take.

During the COVID-19 lockdowns, the Air Quality Index in Delhi dropped by 45% (Garg *et al.*, 2021). In the Greater Beijing–Tianjin–Hebei Region of the PRC also, the nitrogen dioxide levels dropped by as much as 54% (Ghahremanloo *et al.*, 2021). This trend was seen throughout the world. With the economies reopening, however, we can see that pollution levels are increasing and, in some cases, back to the pre-pandemic levels.

What can we learn from this experience? We can and must sustain some of the dramatic changes that we successfully adapted to during the pandemic. Let us take actions to promote a circular economy, apply nature-based solutions, strengthen climate resilience, and live low-carbon lifestyles. Let us build "forward" better. Let us learn from each other and work together in our cities and countries to achieve the 1.5 degree target.

Asia and the Pacific region have been experiencing population rise and economic growth, thus contributing to global GHG emissions. As the region moves beyond the pandemic and into recovery, there must be plans that prioritize climate action to achieve net zero. Recovery planning should focus on three things: people, translating commitments into action, and financing.

## 4.4 An Equitable and Economically Feasible Shift to Net Zero

We are here to discuss how to reach our common vision of an inclusive, net zero, and resilient future. And there are ways Asia and Pacific region can lead in this very important work.

Rising populations and economies contribute considerably to global GHG emissions. But the vulnerability to climate change is growing too. As we try to move beyond the pandemic and into recovery, we must plan now to put climate action front and center. It is an opportunity we cannot miss.

As we observe daily, the Asia–Pacific region continues to grapple with significant health and economic challenges due to COVID-19. While addressing the immediate crisis remains crucial, governments must also remain focused on the climate challenge. The recovery from the pandemic will be a prolonged process. Although, understandably, the short-term emphasis will be on restarting economies and re-employing people, there is also a need for nations to consider longer-term changes that will lead to more sustainable, resilient, and equitable economies and societies.

The global lockdowns in 2020 did lead to a temporary reduction in emissions. However, with economies reopening, there has already been a rebound, with energy-related carbon dioxide emissions rising.

Despite some good work, most governments did not direct COVID-19 stimulus to support green measures. Based on the Vivid Economics' Greenness of Stimulus Index, only 28% of the $17.2 trillion of announced stimulus will go toward sectors that impact climate change, biodiversity, or local air quality (Vivid Economics, 2021).

We must understand that the objectives of addressing climate change and stimulating the economy do not clash. And more broadly, we must know that the transition is a major opportunity. Ambitious climate action can boost economies, create good jobs, and boost health benefits. A return to "business as usual" is not an option. Rather, support for a green, resilient, and inclusive recovery is a key priority.

To do COVID-19 recovery planning and use it as an opportunity to accelerate the needed transition, we need to focus on three things: people, translating commitments into action, and financing (UN *et al.*, 2022).

First, the recovery must be people-centered.

The pandemic is not just a public health crisis. It highlights the many vulnerabilities and recurring socioeconomic gaps. ADB estimates that 78 million people across the Asia–Pacific region have been pushed back into extreme poverty—earning under $1.90/day. If the threshold is increased to $3.20, the number rises to 182 million (ADB, 2021c). In Indonesia alone, by September 2020, there had been an increase of 2.76 million poor people in just one year (BPS, 2021).

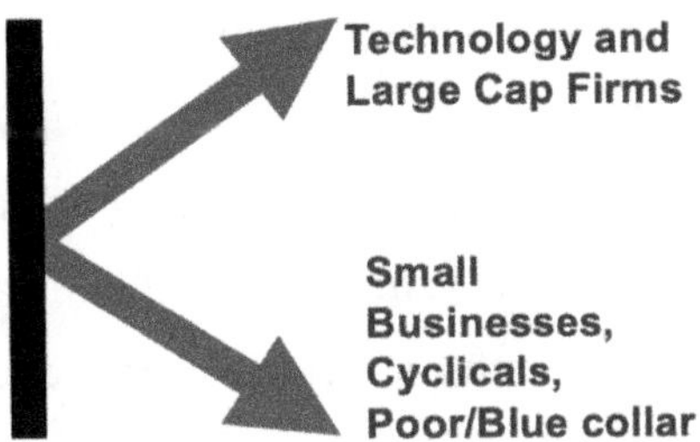



**Figure 4.1** K-Shaped Recovery
Source: Adapted from Gavrilenko (2020).

We must avoid a "k-shaped" recovery—one in which growth trends up for some people and down for others (Figure 4.1). We need to put people at the center of this recovery. We must make the transition just and affordable. And we must focus on building resilience.

Second, we must ensure that commitments turn into action.

It is important to know that we are not at the start of a journey. Countries have progressed and made positive strides in developing national climate plans and policies in line with their Paris Agreement commitments—through nationally determined contributions (NDCs) and national adaptation plans. Multilateral development banks are being asked to raise their ambitions to align with the Paris Agreement. So too must countries raise their NDC ambitions and ensure these commitments translate into action. Whether in energy, transport, industry, or agriculture—and at the national, provincial, local, and community levels, we need a multipronged approach. It will only succeed with strong coordination among institutions and between levels of government.

Finally, we must mobilize sufficient financing.

Sound policies can ensure development follows the right path. But we still need to pay for it. We need an effective menu of financing instruments and mechanisms to reach the level of resources required. We must make the transition affordable and ensure financing flows to those countries that are committed to climate action.

Public financing alone will not be sufficient. For example, just on infrastructure, developing Asia needs to invest $1.7 trillion annually through 2030 to maintain its growth momentum, tackle poverty, and respond to climate change (ADB, 2017b). Scarce public funds, now under added pressure due to COVID-19, must be cleverly used to attract and leverage private sector finance.

Even before the pandemic, markets signaled a shift toward more sustainable and inclusive development. Green finance was flowing into the region. We need to build on this progress and scale up action.

The battle against climate change will be won or lost in Asia and the Pacific region. But we must also remember that the transition to net zero works much better if we reinforce national efforts with regional and global cooperation.

So, let us ask the questions that turn our discussions into action. For example, how do we address the often competing objectives of rapid transition and affordability? How do we foster strong coordination across and within governments? And how do we best use technology to enable action?

Asking hard questions helps build concrete and cooperative actions on the ground. And we cannot delay. We are at a critical juncture with a unique opportunity to pursue a green, resilient, and inclusive recovery. We must be smart. We must be swift. And we must be transformational.

The majority of Asia and the Pacific population lives in coastal areas. The many diverse cultures and traditions are strongly linked to the ocean. In nearly all of the small island states of the Pacific, for example, 90% live within five kilometers of the coast. Preserving oceans becomes crucial as ocean health must be at the heart of the new economy.

## 4.5 Preserving Our Oceans

Oceans are arguably the most important resources and ecosystems for the people of Asia and the Pacific.

The majority of the region's population lives in coastal areas. Many diverse cultures and traditions are strongly linked to the ocean. In nearly all of the small island states of the Pacific, for example, 90% live within five kilometers of the coast (Andrew *et al.*, 2019).

Asia and the Pacific is home to three-quarters of the world's coral reefs and more than half of all remaining mangroves (Abbas, 2023). The Coral Triangle—or "Amazon of the Seas"—is the center of global marine biodiversity. Five of the world's 10 largest fisheries and 90% of its aquaculture are in this region (APEC, 2023; World Bank, 2023b). They are critical to maintaining global food and nutritional security.

The share of the ocean economy to GDP in the region can go as high as 30%, and even 87% in some island nations (Juneja *et al.*, 2021). Over 400 million people in the Bay of Bengal area depend on coastal and marine resources for food, their livelihoods, and security (Christie and Ole-Moiyoi, 2011). This heavy reliance on seas and oceans makes us all extremely vulnerable to any decline or damage to coastal and marine ecosystems.

Our marine ecosystems are now threatened with extinction. Over the past half-century, the world has lost nearly half of its coral reefs and mangrove forests (Marcus, 2018; Wetzel, 2021). More than a third of global fish stocks have been overfished (Parada and Pirlea, 2023). The volume of ocean dead zones—enormous areas where most marine life can no longer survive or breed—continues to expand at an alarming rate (Altieri and Diaz, 2019). The COVID-19 pandemic only worsened the already serious problem of marine plastic pollution.

We must understand just how critical our ocean health is. On average, 30% of a nation's wealth in the region—whether in terms of GDP, exports, or government revenues—comes from natural capital (TEEB, 2010). Protecting our ocean ecosystems is not only an environmental issue, but a development, economic, security, social, and human issue as well.

Our oceans, coastal megacities, and island nations in our region are on the frontlines of climate change. It is encouraging to see momentum building on protecting and restoring our ecosystems. The Global Ocean Alliance now includes 77 countries—17 from Asia and the Pacific—committed to protecting 30% of our global oceans by 2030 (UK Government, n.d.). This is starting to translate into major investments in ecosystems—such as the Sindh Coastal Resilience Project in Pakistan; and better protection and management of 150 km of coastline in Maharashtra in India.

On the global commitment to create a circular economy for plastics, companies producing 20% of all plastic packaging globally have committed to ambitious 2025 targets. A review completed in 2023 showed clear progress in reducing virgin plastic use. But it also stressed that more effort must go toward reducing demand for single-use packaging in the first place (Ellen Macarthur Foundation and UNEP, 2023).

Around the world, ocean-based industries are poised for rapid growth. Estimates show that $2 trillion to $4 trillion in sustainable ocean investments could bring $8 trillion to $23 trillion in net economic benefits (HELP, 2022).

The world is at a critical turning point as we respond to the pandemic and dual climate and biodiversity crises. Ocean health must be at the heart of the so-called "new economy." We must build forward better to both achieve our environmental and climate goals—and create a low-carbon world.

We can build forward better by supporting nature-based solutions, promoting circular economies, mainstreaming blue finance, and ensuring that smallholders and small and medium-sized enterprises—which employ 70% of workers globally—are prioritized (UN *et al.*, 2022; UN, 2024).

Collaboration is essential. Working across sectors is vital.

We all share the vision of a prosperous, inclusive, resilient, and sustainable BLUE future for Asia and the Pacific.

In addition to coastal areas, Asia is also home to many transboundary river basins and experiences many water-related extreme events. The issue of water insecurity, characterized by floods, droughts, and poor water quality, poses significant challenges to this region. The High-Level Experts and Leaders Panel (HELP) principles can help countries prepare and cooperate to build water resilience and foster peace.

## 4.6 Principles to Foster Peace Before, During, and After Water-Related Hazards

Water insecurity comes through floods, drought, and poor water quality. It is either too much, too little, or too polluted water.

According to the World Economic Forum's Global Risks Report 2024, extreme weather is considered the top risk for 2024, likely influenced by the occurrence of the hottest Northern Hemisphere summer on record in 2023. Over the next 10 years, extreme weather events are ranked as the highest global risk that we need to address (World Economic Forum, 2024).

On average, over 20 million people a year are forced from their homes by extreme weather. Weather-related events caused 98% of disaster displacements in 2022—from floods, storms, and wildfires to droughts (IDMC, 2023). They affected highly exposed and densely populated areas.

Asia gets about 70% of these water-related extreme events. It is home to many transboundary river basins—such as the Ganges–Brahmaputra–Meghna basin, the Mekong, the Indus, and Aral Sea (Oregon State University, 2018). In May 2020, cyclone Amphan displaced 5 million people across Bangladesh, India, Myanmar, and Bhutan (UNHCR, 2020). And rising sea levels will increasingly create refugees as people flee low-lying areas.

It is rare, but not uncommon, for water insecurity to be the main cause of conflict. The lack of access to vital resources for food and water can be another reason for conflict. It leads to disagreements, displacement, or instability. However, what is important is that water-related hazards can also create opportunities for peace among riparian countries.

Thus, while water crises can threaten peace if ignored, they can also become the foundation for cooperation and timely, effective policy action. What is needed is an accurate assessment of water-related security risks, so a common knowledge base can be used for creating effective policies through cooperation.

Adopting High-Level Experts and Leaders Panel (HELP) principles to foster peace before, during, and after water-related hazards will also help countries better their relations by jointly overcoming water crises, sharing critical information, and building stronger institutions across shared basins. These principles include (1) enhancing leaders' awareness and actions to foster peace; (2) ensuring the respect of human rights law and international humanitarian law; (3) integrating and linking disaster, natural resources, and crisis management sectors within and among governments; (4) clarifying *ex-ante* the missions of countries and trans-boundary organizations; (5) upgrading existing protocols, agreements, and documents on transboundary cooperation; (6) sharing disaster information; (7) collaborating and coordinating for swift relief and recovery actions; (8) jointly mitigating the impact of disasters; (9) promoting international disaster law; (10) learning from histories, experiences and good practices; and (11) fully using science and technology (HELP Water and Disasters, 2022).

Climate change destabilizes regions, and the loss of nature is another significant destabilizing factor. The Kunming Declaration signed by more than 100 countries during COP15 calls for urgent and integrated action to preserve global biodiversity and protect land and oceans through effective conservation.

Reducing water insecurity—and living in harmony with nature—will help us do better on the Sustainable Development Goals (SDGs) and the UNFCCC 2050 carbon neutrality goal.

One of the initiatives that can leverage community resiliency toward climate change is The Community Resilience Partnership Program (CRPP). CRPP aims to scale up local climate adaptation efforts in the Asia–Pacific region. It focuses on enhancing policy, capacity, and financing to support climate resilience at the community level.

## 4.7 Community Resilience Partnership Program

The Community Resilience Partnership Program (CRPP) is a recent initiative by ADB aimed at expanding local climate adaptation efforts across the Asia–Pacific region (ADB, 2023b). As its name implies, CRPP focuses on community-level climate adaptation measures, which play a crucial role in realizing the goals of the Paris Agreement and Sustainable Development Goals (SDGs).

CRPP has three key features that support countries and communities in the Asia–Pacific region to scale up climate actions at the local level.

First, we need to strengthen policy and capacity in support of local actions on climate resilience. Second, we must scale up climate adaptation action and partnerships to address the nexus of poverty, gender, and climate change. And third, we must find enough climate adaptation finance to meet the needs of the poor and vulnerable populations.

We have already reviewed NDCs and national adaptation plans. The review showed gaps in how climate policies prioritize local action. Thus, it will be critical that CRPP works closely with both national ministries and local governments to develop an evidence base that highlights the importance of investing in local climate adaptation.

For example, CRPP will support governments in integrating community-led adaptation measures into their NDCs and national adaptation plans. It will also help build the capacity of local governments, community groups, and the private sector to deliver climate actions at scale.

Currently, there is a wide gap between national policies and actual action on the ground. This is particularly clear in adaptation measures that explicitly meet the needs of the poor and vulnerable. CRPP will help overcome this barrier in several ways: It will help governments develop large-scale investment projects that support the adaptation needs of the poor and vulnerable. And it will provide grants for piloting innovative solutions at the local level. Examples will be adaptive social protection projects, community-driven climate-resilient development, climate-smart agriculture, disaster resilience microfinance, and risk-informed decentralization.

But we must ensure that the poor population, especially women, are seen as agents of change and are empowered to lead these resilience actions on the ground. Creating innovative partnerships between local governments and grassroots organizations will be critical.

Assessments by the United Nations show that the climate adaptation finance gap is actually widening. Annual global adaptation costs in developing countries alone are estimated to be in the range of $140–$300 billion by 2030 (UNEP, 2021). It is critical that we increase adaptation finance. We also need to ensure that those resources reach the local level to meet local needs. CRPP will help countries and communities build capacity for accessing both domestic and international climate adaptation finance. It will also strengthen partnerships with financial institutions to ensure that downstream investments for projects developed by CRPP have sufficient access to financing.

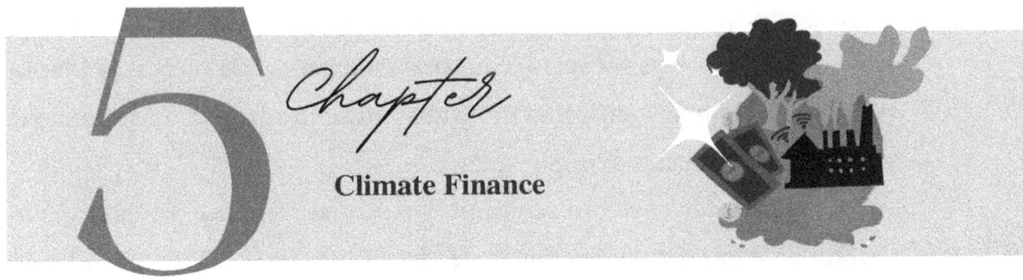



## 5.1 Introduction

Efforts to build climate resilience are essentially linked to climate finance. Climate finance plays a critical role in helping the Asia–Pacific region achieve its ambitious targets for emission reduction. From bustling cities to remote communities, the impacts of climate change are deeply felt, highlighting the need for strategic investment.

Climate finance encompasses a wide range of financial instruments and mechanisms. It can include grants, loans, and other types of financial resources that are directed toward initiatives to address the issue of climate change. Carbon pricing and a climate bank are some component examples of climate finance.

While the need for climate finance has been there for quite a while, the pandemic made things harder by shifting the focus of financial flows from climate issues to more urgent needs. These needs include healthcare and social protection, which directly affect the lives of many people. Because of this shift in priorities for many countries, the pandemic increased investment risks. Therefore, ensuring the availability and adequacy of sustainable climate finance becomes important.

This chapter covers discussions on climate finance, ranging from carbon pricing, nature-positive investment initiatives, climate banks, to sustainable finance. These discussions support the topic of climate resiliency elaborated in Chapter 4 to help address climate change and build forward better.

Asia and the Pacific region are experiencing a growing push toward climate action, with countries setting ambitious targets for emission reduction. Carbon finance—mobilized through international carbon markets—can help countries overcome some barriers to help reach their nationally determined contribution targets.

## 5.2 Implementing Article 6 of the Paris Agreement to Achieve a More Ambitious Goal in Reducing Greenhouse Gas Emissions

Climate change is a global issue. It thus requires a global response and a high level of cooperation. The Asia and the Pacific region currently produces over 50% of global greenhouse (GHG) emissions (Marriott and Aggarwal, 2023). Yet, at the same time, it is creating growing momentum for climate action. Japan and the Republic of Korea are committed to achieving net zero by the middle of the century. The People's Republic of China (PRC) has also set a target of carbon neutrality by 2060 (IISD, 2020).

As we all know, Indonesia has a very large economy and is thus an important player in the battle against climate change. It has also made important commitments to create inclusive, competitive, and sustainable development—all while tackling the impacts of climate change. Indonesia's updated nationally determined contribution (NDC) commits to reducing 31.89% of its GHG emissions unconditionally. It will increase its contribution to 43.2% of GHG emission reductions by 2030, subject to the availability of international support (Republic of Indonesia, 2022). To achieve these goals, Indonesia has implemented Presidential Regulation Number 98, 2021, concerning the Implementation of Carbon Pricing to Achieve the Nationally Determined Contribution Target and Control Over Greenhouse Gas Emissions in the National Development. Additionally, Law Number 7 of 2021 on Harmonization of Tax Regulations introduces a carbon tax to support its national emission trading system for the power sector. Indonesia's biggest utility, Perusahaan Listrik Negara, has pledged to phase out fossil fuels by 2060 to achieve carbon neutrality (PLN, 2022).

These announcements and commitments to decarbonize and change energy production are most promising. But the real question is, how can we ensure these ambitious plans translate into immediate action or real projects on the ground?

There are many barriers to producing real climate action. They include collecting and disseminating good information. There are economic, financial, investment, and legal barriers as well (ADB, 2023c). One of the most important is access to climate finance. Yet, the lack of access to climate finance remains and will continue to remain a major hurdle to effectively tackling climate change. It is in this context that carbon finance—mobilized through international carbon markets—can help countries like Indonesia overcome some of these barriers and help achieve their NDC targets.

Why is Article 6 so important? For one, it establishes a new framework for international carbon markets and can play a key role in advancing climate action and ambition (ADB, 2023c). It can also help Indonesia meet its NDC targets cost-effectively and increase its climate ambition over time to find ways to achieving net zero emissions. Article 6 opens a window for mobilizing carbon finance and thus scale up the adoption of advanced low-carbon technologies. Indonesia's NDC recognizes the strategic importance of Article 6.

Indonesia holds significant expertise on how to make international carbon markets work. Under the Clean Development Mechanism, Indonesia hosted over 150 projects and programs (ADB, 2021d). It was also very early in using the Joint Crediting Mechanism, which is considered by many to be the forerunner to Article 6.2. The challenge now is to leverage all of this knowledge and experience to operationalize and take advantage of the new market mechanisms under Article 6.

> Countries must align pandemic recovery plans with their NDCs to achieve mitigation goals and foster sustainable growth. Carbon pricing is central to broader climate policy by mobilizing finance for green recovery. This simply means that polluting air is not free.

## 5.3 Unlocking Green Recovery: Harnessing Carbon Pricing for Sustainable Growth in Vulnerable Economies

When designing pandemic recovery packages, countries need to transform their high-carbon development plans to align with their NDCs under the Paris Agreement and create ambitious mitigation goals. To do this, we need green recovery plans that restrict GHG levels and build resilience. This will contribute to a more inclusive economic recovery with sustainable growth.

The arguments for a green recovery are compelling. And they are especially relevant for the Vulnerable Group of 20 (V20) countries. But to do this, these vulnerable countries need both internal and external finance. This is where carbon pricing can play a major role in mobilizing additional resources.

Carbon pricing is central to the broader climate policy architecture. It can help countries meet emission reduction targets cost-effectively (ADB, 2022e). This simply means that air pollution is not free. When implemented in tandem with other policies, carbon pricing can bring substantial gains to both the economy and the environment.

Carbon pricing instruments such as carbon taxes or emission trading systems (ETS) can create additional domestic revenue (ADB, 2022e). These can be earmarked to fund mitigation actions and drive low-carbon innovation and the technology needed to further support a green recovery and sustainable growth. Carbon pricing also directly attracts investment and helps disseminate advanced low-carbon technologies. These can be crucial for green growth, again very relevant in the current context for V20 countries.

The V20 can also mobilize carbon finance using international carbon markets, especially those envisaged under Article 6 of the Paris Agreement.

There is increased impetus and momentum in the region to establish carbon pricing systems. Globally, there are 75 carbon pricing instruments in operation (World Bank, 2024b). In 2024, carbon taxes and emission trading systems (ETS) covered 24% of global GHG emissions (World Bank, 2024b). There are several carbon pricing initiatives implemented at the national level in Asia and the Pacific; Japan and Singapore employ a carbon tax; Australia, Kazakhstan, New Zealand, Indonesia, the Republic of Korea, and PRC have launched an ETS (Climate Governance Initiative, 2024; World Bank, 2023c). Malaysia, Vietnam, and Thailand are all considering options for ETS (World Bank, 2023c).

Among V20 countries, Vietnam has issued the revised "Law on Environmental Protection," which requires the Ministry of Natural Resources and Environment (MONRE) and the Ministry of Finance to develop a national crediting mechanism (NCM) and a domestic ETS (ICAP, 2024a). The Philippines' House of Representatives Committee on Climate Change also conditionally approved the "Low Carbon Economy Act of 2022," which includes provisions for an ETS to achieve national targets (ICAP, 2024b). Almost all V20 countries have experience in hosting baseline-and-crediting mechanisms—such as the Clean Development Mechanism and the Joint Crediting Mechanism. Half of the V20 have expressed interest in using market mechanisms to achieve their NDCs.

Finally, I would like to urge those who have initiated or already implemented carbon pricing schemes to keep up the momentum. They should continue planning and remain committed to implementation. This will help achieve a green recovery and stimulate green growth. I also urge those who have not done so yet to explore ways of harnessing the benefits of carbon pricing.

ASEAN members have the opportunity to use Article 6 of the Paris Agreement as an additional source of finance. International carbon market mechanisms can support and enhance domestic carbon pricing initiatives, leading to more emission reduction.

## 5.4 Carbon Pricing for ASEAN

Carbon pricing is a key element in the policy mix to meet climate goals under the Paris Agreement. Accordingly, we have seen an increase in the number of carbon pricing initiatives that support national emission-reduction goals. Globally, there are 75 carbon pricing instruments, with carbon taxes and ETS covering about 24% of global GHG emissions (World Bank, 2024b).

The ASEAN region, home to over 650 million people, is one of the world's fastest-growing economic areas. However, this rapid economic growth has come with a significant environmental cost, as ASEAN is also among the top greenhouse gas emitters globally, primarily due to its energy sector. The region contributes around 7% of global GHG emissions, with the energy industry responsible for more than 60% of these emissions (ASEAN, 2023a). With five of the world's 20 most climate-vulnerable countries located in ASEAN, the region faces serious risks from climate change. If climate change continues unchecked, it could reduce the region's GDP by 11% by 2100 and displace 87 million people in high-risk flood areas across Indonesia, Malaysia, Myanmar, Thailand, and Vietnam (ASEAN, 2023b).

At present, Singapore and Indonesia are the only ASEAN countries with established carbon pricing policies. However, the innovative efforts of Brunei, the ongoing progress in Cambodia and Vietnam, along with Thailand's and Malaysia's plans to explore carbon taxes and ETS, highlight that ASEAN nations are actively developing carbon pricing policies and demonstrating various approaches and levels of ambition (Rakhiemah *et al.*, 2024). Table 5.1 outlines the status of carbon pricing in ASEAN as of February 2024.

ASEAN members hold the opportunity to use Article 6 of the Paris Agreement as an additional source of finance. They may want to examine how international carbon market mechanisms support and enhance domestic carbon pricing initiatives. In the longer term, they can look at how pricing schemes can link up. Using international carbon markets can lead to significant cost reductions and provide an additional source of revenue for both ASEAN governments and their private sectors.

**Table 5.1** Status of Carbon Pricing in ASEAN Countries

| Countries | Net Zero Target | Carbon Pricing in Climate Change Policy | Carbon Tax | Emission Trading System (ETS) | Carbon Credit |
|---|---|---|---|---|---|
| Brunei Darussalam | Net Zero 2050 | V | X | X | X |
| Cambodia | Carbon Neutral 2050 | X | X | X | V |
| Indonesia | Net Zero 2060 or sooner | V | X | V | V |
| Lao PDR | Net Zero 2050 | X | X | X | V |
| Malaysia | Carbon Neutral 2050 | V | X | X | V |
| Myanmar | Net Zero from Forestry and Other Land Use 2040 | X | X | X | V |
| Philippines | No target set | V | X | X | V |
| Singapore | Net Zero 2050 | V | V | X | V |
| Thailand | Carbon Neutral 2050; Net Zero 2065 | V | X | X | V |
| Vietnam | Net Zero 2050 | V | X | X | V |

Source: Adapted from Rakhiemah et al. (2024).

Dialogue and sharing experiences bring countries at different stages of familiarity and knowledge on carbon pricing and markets together. ASEAN holds the potential to be epicenter of the next generation of carbon pricing and carbon market mechanisms.

Asia and the Pacific region are rich in biodiversity but face increasing pressure impacting food security, livelihoods, and public health. Green bonds, blue bonds, and a "nature-positive investment road map" are some financing tools and initiatives to support nature and biodiversity projects.

## 5.5 Pathways Toward a Nature-Positive Future

Asia and the Pacific region have some of our planet's richest concentrations of biological diversity. It is home to 17 of the world's 36 biodiversity hotspots and seven of its 17 megadiverse countries (IPBES, 2018). But they are all coming under increasing stress with a critical impact on food security, livelihoods, public health, and disaster resilience.

To aid developing nations in Asia and the Pacific in promoting environmental stewardship and mitigating biodiversity loss, strategic initiatives have been implemented to provide innovative financing for nature and biodiversity projects. This includes direct financing and credit enhancement, along with other financial instruments such as green bonds, blue bonds, blended finance, and public–private partnerships (ADB, 2022f).

For instance, in collaboration with bilateral partners, initiatives like the Biodiversity Conservation Corridors Initiative in the Greater Mekong Subregion have been devised and executed to address ecosystem fragmentation across seven transboundary biodiversity landscapes (ADB, 2014). Efforts are underway to establish public–private partnerships for Coral Reef Finance and Insurance in Asia and the Pacific, while endeavors to bolster ocean preservation have been reinforced through the issuance of dual-tranche blue bonds denominated in Australian and New Zealand dollars (ADB, 2021e; GEF, 2021).

Furthermore, a comprehensive "nature-positive investment road map" is being developed to provide strategic guidance on valuing and incorporating nature into decision-making processes (ADB, 2022g). This roadmap aims to facilitate the scaling up of nature-positive investments in operational activities and assist member countries in transitioning toward nature-positive decision-making. The objective is to augment the global availability of natural assets, foster a green recovery post-pandemic, and generate more environmentally sustainable employment opportunities.

The road map will also help mainstream biodiversity and nature-based solutions in infrastructure projects—whether in transport, seaports, energy, water, telecommunications, and urban development. It will be supported by a natural capital lab that will incubate, accelerate, and expand natural capital investments using natural capital accounting, payments for ecosystem services, and blended finance.

An outcome of these efforts is the creation of the innovative Natural Capital Financing Facility, aimed at enhancing the resilience and sustainability of nature-dependent food systems in the long term (ADB, 2021f). This initiative also aims to bolster oceanic health through sustainable tourism and fisheries while safeguarding and restoring critical ecosystems. Moreover, support is extended to initiatives like the Regional Flyway Initiative, aimed at preserving wildlife habitats, sustaining ecosystem services, and providing livelihoods for millions of individuals (ADB, 2023d).

As the COVID-19 pandemic evolves, it has become a wake-up call from nature—that integral nexus between humans, animals, and nature coexisting on one planet.

Let us all work together, strengthen our partnerships, and work toward preserving Mother Earth!

Preserving nature is increasingly being included in climate change actions. Initiatives like the Natural Capital Financing Facility and the Regional Flyway Initiatives are examples of efforts to support nature-positive investments and protect vital ecosystems.

## 5.6 Assessing Natural Capital and Realizing the Value of Ecological Products

The Ecological Civilization Forum offers an opportunity to break new ground in stopping and reversing the rapid decline in biodiversity and the ecosystems that are our natural capital.

Natural capital is critical to our existence. We must value nature—with all its complexity and diversity—as the foundation of all human activity. Nature is vitally important to our health and wealth. It helps us adapt to and mitigate climate change. And it serves as a buffer against future pandemics.

We still struggle to highlight the role nature plays in crafting our development and investment agendas. One reason is that we do not sufficiently value what natural capital contributes to our economies. We tend to undervalue nature and leave it out of economic and financial decision-making.

We must integrate and "price" nature into development planning, policymaking, financial reform, investment planning, and knowledge generation. We need to elevate nature into our decision-making processes.

Taking a nature-positive approach, we include nature-related risks when making management and investment decisions. This will ensure we avoid or minimize negative effects and help restore and expand natural capital.

How can we support the transition to nature-positive investments? We explore the complexities of natural capital accounting, looking for innovative ways to value nature as we continue to seek a green, nature-positive, inclusive, resilient, and sustainable economic recovery.

A regional natural capital lab (NCL) has been established to aid developing countries in evaluating natural capital, fortifying regulatory frameworks, and employing innovative financing to bolster investments that promote nature positivity. Led by the One-ADB NCL working group, the NCL serves as a platform for advancing these objectives (ADB, 2022g).

A key initiative is the Innovative Natural Capital Financing Facility, which focuses on strengthening the long-term resilience and sustainability of food systems reliant on nature (ADB, 2021f). It also promotes ocean health by investing in nature-friendly projects within sustainable tourism and fisheries, while protecting and restoring vital ecosystems. Moreover, it supports efforts like the Regional Flyway Initiative, which preserves wildlife habitats, maintains essential ecosystem services, and supports the livelihoods of millions of people (ADB, 2023d).

As we engage in discussions on knowledge solutions with development partners, we will spotlight the tools that have emerged from our collaborative efforts to accurately assess nature's value. Moreover, we will explore avenues to refine and integrate these tools into everyday practices.

Asia and the Pacific need a strong climate bank to adopt new and innovative strategies to address climate change. A climate bank would offer affordable financing, multiple financing instruments, and a pipeline of bankable climate change projects, mobilizing resources to meet long-term development goals and ambitious net-zero targets.

## 5.7 Why Asia and the Pacific Needs a Strong Climate Bank

For those who followed the 2021 United Nations Climate Change Conference, or COP26, in Glasgow, the headlines may not have been too encouraging. Yet, behind the scenes, it was climate finance that took center stage. For Asia and the Pacific, it all seemed to point to the need for a strong climate bank.

Let's start with why Asia and the Pacific? There are three typical reasons. First, Asia and the Pacific is home to many of the small island development states. Given the unique scattered geography and often coral-based ecosystems—in many instances, just a few meters above sea level—climate change is a clear existential threat. From the Maldives in the Indian Ocean to the Marshall Islands in the middle of the Pacific Ocean, if we can't contain global warming, these countries may simply disappear in another 50 years.

Second, the region gets pummeled by natural disasters more than most. From droughts to floods, typhoons, cyclones, and other extreme weather events, each year there are lives lost, property and infrastructure destroyed, and economies disrupted. In the Philippines, for example, damage from extreme weather and disasters reached the equivalent of $9.3 billion from 2010 to 2019 (Mapa, 2020). For a small island state that loses its port, it becomes isolated even more. It exemplifies the antifragility theme as described by Nassim Nicholas Taleb. Without a functioning port to deliver basic goods, people's survival becomes at risk.

Third, Asia and the Pacific accounts for about half of all global greenhouse gas (GHG) emissions (Marriott and Aggarwal, 2023). This is not only due to the region's large population but also because Asia has become a global manufacturing base, and home to a large share of carbon-fired energy plants. Fossil fuels continue to dominate. Of the 1,002 coal-fired plants planned or under construction worldwide, 865 are in the Asia–Pacific (Fujitsu, 2022). We need a "just" transition out of coal. And the region does have many alternative resources, with several governments actively pursuing them. It is often said that the Battle of Climate Change will be won or lost in Asia.

Developing countries in the region need three basic things to mitigate and adapt to climate change (ADB, 2019b). First are the technical solutions they can apply to projects that green their economies. Second is the expertise and capacity to collaborate and coordinate across government and the private sector to approach climate change holistically. The critical third part is the financial resources to build new and transform existing infrastructure, expand climate literacy and training, and produce innovative solutions that respond to the local environment and acknowledge local conditions. Taken together, it produces a "solutions ++" approach—a solution that embeds active knowledge (the first "+") and finance (the second). A demand-driven climate bank with experience spanning half a century should fit the bill.

Technical solutions require the knowledge gleaned over the years when testing the feasibility and designing climate change development projects. Then an appropriate package of loans, investments, guarantees, and grants that can attract the right partners must be assembled. Climate change mitigation and adaptation add value by preserving ecosystems and reducing carbon footprints. Technical assistance boosts capacity in building overall awareness, increasing understanding, and providing local ownership of the projects themselves. It is essential that people understand how best to invest in the climate change agenda. Ultimately, it helps boost productivity. That's why it's important to have a climate bank that can work with developing countries to design climate solutions that have a greater impact, and move toward more ambitious Paris Agreement NDC through meaningful projects linked to a country's national development strategy. How to provide adequate power while tackling climate change is different for each country. The alternative renewable energy mix—whether wind farms or solar parks—can add to hydropower or geothermal generation that is less dirty and contributes to the energy transition process. It all depends on what's available.

Similarly, technical expertise supports the transfer of new technologies that allow greater access to power as well as promote the energy transition. This is critical to a region where 150 million people cannot access electricity and another 350 million have unreliable access (ADB, 2024b). Capacity development also helps countries formulate a just transition through vocational training and social development, so these investments do not disrupt income growth or safety nets for the more vulnerable segments of the population.

Without this awareness, capacity development, and ownership, it would not be possible to develop a pipeline of ambitious and robust, green and resilient, nature-positive investment projects. A climate bank must be able to work with its partners and clients to drive new ideas on how to, for example, better manage coastal wetlands to contain surges and floods and act as natural sponges to absorb flooding rather than building conventional seawalls.

A climate bank, of course, has the fundamental responsibility of offering affordable financing with competitive lending rates—from either concessional or quasi-concessional sources with relatively long tenors (ADB, 2023c). Strong balance sheets and high credit ratings do not come overnight but are nonetheless essential for this to happen. A climate bank can also use multiple financing instruments, including guarantees, to leverage resources and serve as an important conduit for co-financing.

Ultimately, however, what distinguishes a climate bank from finance institutions is a pipeline of bankable climate change projects with upfront due diligence, prefeasibility, and other preparatory work. Projects evolve through careful structuring to ensure the economic and financial returns are income-generating and welfare-enhancing and can attract commercial financing. A pipeline of climate bank investment projects must mobilize a blended mix of commercial, official development assistance, and grants that can be leveraged multiple times. Climate financing must be sufficiently large to help meet long-term development strategies while reaching ambitious net zero targets by mid-century.

Adding knowledge and finance to bankable pipelines provides climate solutions. A climate bank can combine and translate these tangible and intangible assets into partnership facilities or trust funds. Building on a credible record of past commitments, these have a higher climate change development impact. To paraphrase Mohamed El Erian, an economist and a former CEO of PIMCO, if we are to succeed in tackling the climate change crisis, climate banks might just be the major game in town.

> As Asia and the Pacific moves into pandemic recovery, the challenge of mobilizing sustainable climate finance has become a major priority. This is particularly true in mounting a low-carbon transition. The pandemic increased investment risk, and we all have the responsibility to steer financial flows toward sustainable investments despite the pandemic.

## 5.8 Scaling Up Sustainable Finance for a Low-Carbon Transition

The pandemic continues to disrupt our lives and economies. But with increased vaccinations and continued policy support, we are cautiously moving into a recovery phase. As we do this, we must now plan to put climate action front and center in our recovery strategies.

In many ways, Asia is at the frontline of climate change. It is the world's most exposed region to disasters and climate risk. For two decades, almost 40% of disasters globally occurred in Asia and the Pacific (UNEP, 2017). This growing vulnerability means we must increase efforts to build resilience and close the financing gap to fight climate change. Also, Asia–Pacific is responsible for as much as 51% of annual global carbon and GHG emissions (Marriott and Aggarwal, 2023).

Effectively managing climate change risks will help shape the recovery. I would like to stress two important facts about battling climate change (ADB, 2019b):

- First, we must recognize how the climate change agenda benefits development. Rather than holding back economic progress and global growth, climate mitigation and adaptation is an opportunity to mobilize capital, skills, and new actors in support of development. We should use the recovery to recalibrate our priorities, align with long-term emission targets, and build resilience.
- Second, as we decarbonize globally, we must create an environment that attracts more people and institutions to support public and private initiatives. It is critical we respond to local circumstances. COP26 helped define a road map to do this, with new initiatives and strong commitments from the private sector.

Let me share some thoughts from my participation at COP26.

COP26 reaffirmed just how essential it is to catalyze global efforts to attain the environmental agenda. Countries agreed to a range of commitments to meet NDCs. These included reaching net-zero emissions, phasing down fossil fuels, tackling deforestation, increasing adaptation measures, and adopting clean technologies.

It was clear through the detailed negotiations and final statement that more needs to be done—more financing, more innovation, and more collaboration.

Many countries in the region are adopting policies that promote a low-carbon transition. They encourage diversifying energy sources, producing more clean energy, and using new technologies to make electricity affordable and create green jobs. Energy policy should take a holistic approach to carbon markets by mobilizing international carbon finance through trust funds and technical support.

We must craft strategies to attract investments that steer us to a low-carbon trajectory. Clearly, the capital needed is well beyond what the public sector can provide. Developing Asia needs to invest $1.7 trillion a year to maintain growth momentum, end poverty, and address climate change (ADB, 2017b). Given the fiscal impact of the pandemic, we need to mobilize even more private capital.

Fortunately, sustainable finance is growing rapidly across the region. Asia now has the second largest regional sustainable bond market after Europe, with about 30% of the global green bonds market (Figure 5.1). Institutional investors want to hedge or mitigate sustainability risks and build greater resilience for the future.

Stakeholder preferences are changing too. Approximately more than one-third of all assets under management (AUM) are now subject to some form of environment, social, and governance (or environmental, social, and governance (ESG)) framework. Global ESG assets are on track to exceed US$40 trillion by 2030 (Bloomberg Intelligence, 2024).

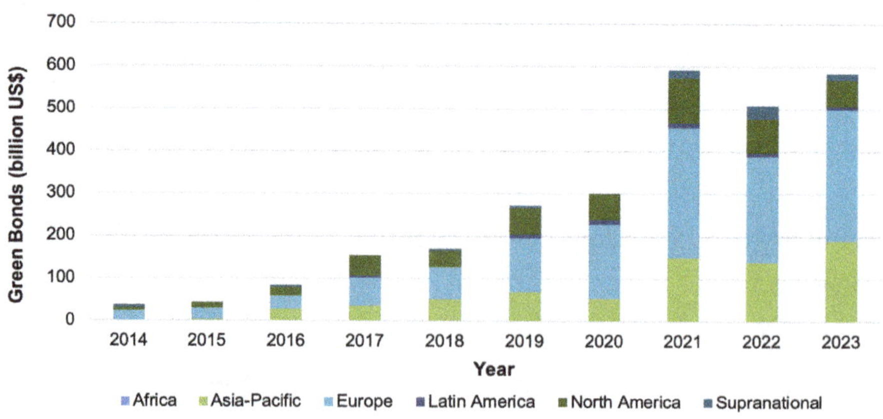


**Figure 5.1** Global Green Bonds Value (2014–2023)
Source: Adapted from Statista (2024c).

Sustainable finance offers new opportunities to the private sector. Companies with high ESG standards are generally associated with better financial results, operational efficiency, and innovation (Chen *et al.*, 2023). They weather the pandemic better. They attract and retain talent. Reputation and customer loyalty are also benefits for those adopting ESG frameworks.

One example is Ganesha, a recycling company in India committed to plastic pollution–free cities (Ganesha Ecosphere, 2018). Its value increased significantly with a positive re-rating by investors. Another example is City Development Limited, Singapore's top real estate company, which reduced carbon emissions by 42% since 2007 (CDL, 2022). Its ESG-centric vision allowed it to tap green financing and expand operations. TSMC, a semiconductor leader, just committed to reaching net zero emissions by 2050.

Yet, we must improve the ESG regulatory framework. Multiple reporting standards are a major barrier. And the surge in ESG products could lead to greenwashing, which requires more financial supervision. Better ESG data and third-party certification can help stop faking.

In July 2021, the G20 pledged to promote mandatory climate-related financial disclosures to create a baseline global reporting standard (Italian G20 Presidency, 2021). Asia must join the discussion to help build common taxonomies, standards, reporting, and information disclosure.

Policymakers should also incorporate sustainability risk into their micro- and macro-prudential frameworks. They can strengthen market infrastructure by mitigating investor risk, smoothing cash flow, securing investible grade ratings, and offering credit guarantees for borrowers. They can tap long-term capital such as pension and insurance companies and introduce green foreign direct investment standards.

The potential to reduce GHG emissions is huge in Asia and the Pacific.

Governments are also developing national climate plans aligned with their Paris Agreement commitments—through NDCs and national adaptation plans.

It is now time to turn these commitments into action.

This requires, for example, reducing GHG emissions, adopting low-carbon technologies, and mobilizing carbon finance, among others.

The review of NDCs and national adaptation plans highlighted the gaps in how a country's climate policies prioritize local action. We need to ensure that mobilized resources meet local needs and the priorities of the poor and vulnerable.

To do so, we must scale up climate adaptation and foster resilience. None of these goals can be achieved without adequate, quality infrastructure. We need greater investment in infrastructure that is environmentally sustainable, low-carbon, climate-resilient, and—importantly—meets the needs of the local community.

The pandemic increased investment risk, making it particularly difficult to mobilize financing for green infrastructure. Adopting low-carbon technologies and building green infrastructure requires significant upfront fixed costs. Up to 65% of Asia's infrastructure projects are not considered bankable (ADB, 2021g). We need more innovative financing instruments and platforms to attract private investment. Greater support from private sector partners is needed to make climate finance commercially attractive.

We all have a responsibility to steer financial flows toward sustainable investments (ADB, 2022f).

First, governments must work with regional and multilateral bodies to internationally harmonize regulatory regimes and promote common standards of information disclosure and impact measurement. Together, policymakers can foster a new ecosystem that incorporates sustainability risk, taps new investors, and promotes stakeholder engagement, while ensuring financial stability.

Second, investors, rating providers, and market participants have a key role in shaping sustainable finance. We need to encourage them to adopt strategies that reward disclosure and meet sustainability goals. Transparent metrics in carbon emissions, environmental R&D, and use of renewable energy will be essential for impact measurement and management.

Finally, Asian firms have the potential to create long-term sustainable value. For this, they must build a robust sustainability strategy, reassess business operations, adopt stronger governance standards, introduce new risk management practices, and improve reporting and communication.

Ambitious national climate commitments must be met for the region to achieve a green, resilient, and inclusive recovery from the pandemic. Tackling climate change is integral to sustainable development. And mobilizing capital for a low-carbon transition is a great opportunity for the region to reach a low-carbon future. We must continue to innovate and create new ways to make this happen.

# 6

## Chapter

**Connectivity:
Infrastructure and
Transportation**

## 6.1 Introduction

In just about every way, the pandemic was anathema to connectivity. During lockdowns, transportation systems were stymied. People simply couldn't go out. Everything had to be delivered. Cross-border mobility (tourism) stopped. Supply chains, both domestic and international, were all eventually affected. Grounded airlines needed financial aid.

But in the face of this adversity, there continues to be great innovation. People and transportation systems adapted. New, more efficient, and safer means to deliver food and other goods developed, mostly because digitalized commerce was already rapidly expanding before the pandemic struck. The pandemic accelerated the trend. As restrictions on mobility gradually eased, most changes were not simply kept, but they continued to innovate and change to meet the new demand under new circumstances.

There is a much bigger picture here, however. Adequate, accessible, environmentally sustainable public and private sector financed infrastructure impacts every aspect of an economy. Connectivity matters just as much for markets as it does for rapidly urbanizing societies. It matters for education and health services. And it significantly matters as we build forward more climate-resilient green systems.

The sections in this chapter cover all these elements, from basic transportation and road safety to supply chain development. It discusses the financing challenges as new infrastructure becomes ever more costly, for example, using land value capture or making green infrastructure more "bankable." It discusses infrastructure governance, and how expanding trade can drive better and more efficient connectivity. Most importantly, it shows how well-thought-out, environmentally sound, and well-designed projects are essential to achieve a future of sustainable and inclusive growth across Asia and the Pacific.

> In Asia and the Pacific, high-quality, fiscally sustainable infrastructure helps drive growth and poverty alleviation. Yet currently, the region suffers from significant infrastructure deficits, not just by quantity, but in terms of quality and accessibility as well.

## 6.2 Infrastructure for Sustainable and Inclusive Growth

Infrastructure is more than an explicit goal of the 2030 sustainable development agenda; it is also a key enabler. As depicted in Figure 6.1, the Asian Development Bank (ADB, 2017b) published a study in 2017 that showed that—to maintain current growth momentum—we needed $26 trillion in infrastructure investment by 2030. That translates into some $1.7 trillion per year. Substantial public and private investments are required to narrow

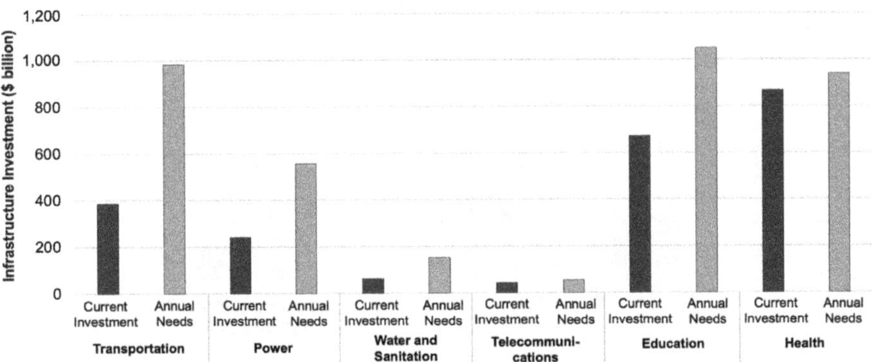

**Figure 6.1** Infrastructure Challenges in Asia and the Pacific: Infrastructure Investment—Current and Projected by Sector ($ Billion)

Notes:
1. For Transportation, Power, Water and Sanitation, Telecommunications: Current Investment is based on 2011 figures. Investment needs are for 2016–2030 divided by 15 years.
2. For Education and Health. Figures only include 18 DMCs. Year coverage: 2009 (Education) and 2013 (Health) for the Philippines; 2013 for Fiji, India, Thailand, and Viet Nam; 2014 for Armenia, Bangladesh, Bhutan, Indonesia, Nepal, Pakistan, Sri Lanka, and Timor-Leste; 2011 (Education) and 2014 (Health) for Mongolia; 2015 (Education) and 2014 (Health) for Kazakhstan; 2014 for the Kyrgyz Republic; 2012 for Georgia; and 2012 (Education) and 2014 (Health) for the People's Republic of China.

Source: Adapted from ADB (2017b).

the gaps. Figure 6.2 highlights the significant infrastructure financing gap across Asia and the Pacific, revealing the critical need to attract additional private sector resources to supplement limited public funding. It is increasingly clear that there is insufficient fiscal space or capacity to mobilize the required external resources to publicly finance this infrastructure. Thus, we must attract and leverage additional private sector resources through strategic and creative use of those available from the public sector.

The pandemic is fundamentally changing the ability of governments to fulfill infrastructure needs. The collapse in economic activity slashed revenues. It put pressure on routine expenditures as well as other critical spending—most notably for social support, education, and healthcare. Governments spent about 8% of GDP on income support. This leaves much less room for public infrastructure spending.

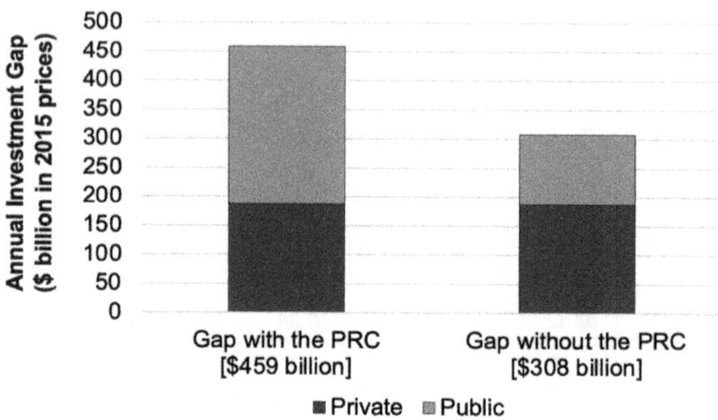


**Figure 6.2** Infrastructure Challenges in Asia and the Pacific: Financing Gap—Public versus Private, 2016–2020

Notes: PRC = People's Republic of China; Number may not add up to total due to rounding.
Source: Adapted from ADB (2017b).

In response, a regional hub is being established to facilitate domestic resource mobilization and international tax cooperation. Its objective is to assist countries in fortifying their revenue sources and extending taxation to burgeoning economic sectors, including the digital economy and e-commerce. Infrastructure governance is perceived as a collaborative endeavor.

The following are three fundamental and universally applicable components (ADB and ADB Institute, 2009; ADB, 2017b).

The first is that hard, physical infrastructure investment is as much about mobilizing resources as it is about better management. This includes a better balance between the design and implementation of new greenfield projects and investments in brownfield projects. Strengthening the maintenance of existing infrastructure assets is critical—whether retrofitting or climate-proofing, for example. Too often the lack of operational or maintenance support ends up undermining value for money.

Second, the so-called "soft" components of project design and filters can raise any project's quality. Quality assurance assesses and mitigates against increasing risks. This works for both standard construction or operational risks and the broader socioeconomic risks—such as integrity, poverty, inequality, and climate change. This requires better collaboration between procurement, financial management, safeguards, monitoring and evaluation, and stakeholder participation.

Finally, building on what we know and increasing capacity goes together with transparency and accountability. It does not happen mechanically. It happens by strengthening the ability of government agencies to understand and apply governance principles, particularly those associated with quality infrastructure investment.

Let me conclude by stressing that the governance of infrastructure has never been more relevant. Financing combined with technical assistance across all levels of government will make infrastructure investments more efficient, sustainable, and inclusive.

> Providing adequate infrastructure in urban areas is very crucial. Land value capture (LVC) can serve as an alternative financing mechanism to support infrastructure development as well as a tool to help cities become an engine of growth. LVC creates a cycle of funding through property value appreciation. Developing Asia can benefit greatly from applying land value capture, especially as we move into a post-pandemic recovery.

## 6.3 Value Capture Infrastructure Financing

Understanding the importance of value capture is essential for anyone involved in urban development. Value capture is not just a mechanism for financing infrastructure. It is a tool that helps make cities an engine of growth—one that requires good urban planning and management.

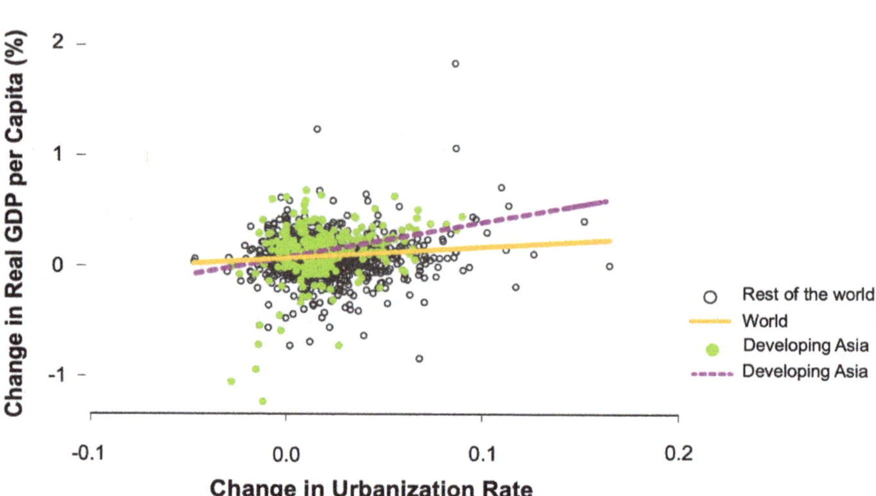



**Figure 6.3** Change in Real GDP Per Capita and Urbanization Rate
Source: Adapted from ADB (2019c).

Urbanization feeds economic growth in a two-way process. In developing Asia, countries that urbanize faster tend to see faster per capita GDP growth (Figure 6.3). While growth promotes urbanization, cities also promote economic growth (ADB, 2019c).

How does this work?

Cities increase productivity through several channels, collectively known as agglomeration economies. And as productivity increases, more firms and households are drawn into cities, increasing their size. Unfortunately, if urban infrastructure does not keep up—using good urban planning to ensure affordable housing and sanitation, for example—the result is congestion, or worse, gridlock.

Transport is central for keeping congestion in check and allowing cities to produce more. Several studies show that productivity is higher in cities where workers can access a larger number of job opportunities—over a reasonable time frame (Bertaud, 2015). A study from the Republic of Korea suggests that a 10% increase in jobs accessible to workers within an hour's travel time is associated with a 2.4% increase in labor productivity (Prud'homme and Lee, 1998). This shows how vital it is for cities to develop fast, affordable, and integrated transport systems.

However, a key challenge is that such infrastructure can be very expensive. For example, according to a recent assessment of metro systems in Asia, the cost per kilometer of modern metro lines has ranged from $33 million to $166 million, and the total cost would be anything between $3 billion and $5 billion (Clark, 2021). Other sectors are no different—water supply and sanitation systems are also very costly (Hutton and Varughese, 2016). So, how do we finance these huge sums?

Essentially, to meet its infrastructure needs, a country needs to both increase its infrastructure investments in a big way and to do so, increasingly rely on private sector finance—particularly innovative sources of finance.

This is where land value capture (LVC) comes in. LVC can create a virtuous cycle (ADB, 2021h). It allows cities to fund and roll out over many years a widespread transport network, along with other core infrastructure. For example, investments in mass transit improve accessibility and thus raise property values. If a portion of this value increase is invested in expanding the network further, accessibility and property values will continue to rise.

This type of mass transit funding goes back more than a century. We saw how LVC was integral in funding urban transport networks in Japan, the Republic of Korea, the People's Republic of China, Hong Kong, and Singapore. It has proven sustainable over the years and even decades.

In India, there is a study on how LVC frameworks can be used across various cities (ADB, 2022h). For example, the study is pointing at the

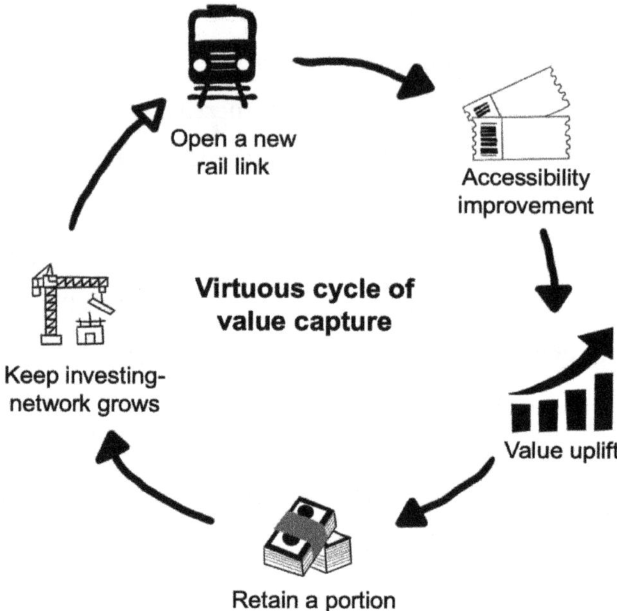


**Figure 6.4** Land Value Capture as a Key Part of Solution
Source: Adapted from ADB (2021h).

possibility that low floor area ratios in Bangalore may limit the full benefits associated with mass transit systems. In the Philippines, spatial comput-able general equilibrium modeling is being used to understand how firms and households in southern Luzon will respond to a new North–South Commuter Rail project (JICA, 2018; Railway Technology, 2024). This study in the Philippines can help model the policy and project impact—including that of the planned Metro-Manila subway project.

Lastly, let me emphasize that we need to exploit the full potential of tools such as LVC financing, especially today when the COVID-19 pandemic is constraining the availability of public finances. As illustrated in Figure 6.4, Asia can benefit greatly by applying land value capture, especially as we move into a post-pandemic recovery.

The world still faces a massive financing gap for investment in new and existing infrastructure, which could generate a serious bottleneck to economic growth and development in the future. This G20 workshop examined how multilateral development banks can help design green infrastructure projects that reduce risk and thus become more "bankable."

## 6.4 Digitalization and Well-Prepared Projects

This is a very timely opportunity to discuss progress in the collaboration among multilateral development banks (MDBs) in helping to promulgate the G20 Principles for Quality Infrastructure Investment (QII).

Meeting the infrastructure financing gap, while achieving the Sustainable Development Goals (SDGs), is more relevant today than ever. Even before COVID-19, ADB had estimated the infrastructure needs of Asia and the Pacific to be around $1.7 trillion a year by 2030, or about 5% of the regional GDP (ADB, 2017b). The pandemic has since compounded the challenge of addressing humanitarian and socioeconomic issues in communities that are already exposed to climate change and natural disasters.

In developing and developed economies alike, governments initiate the formulation of infrastructure project proposals that are critical to closing the infrastructure gap and achieving the SDGs. Yet, beyond public funds, substantially more innovative and private sector financing sources are needed to meet the vast infrastructure needs. We can say that this need has become more acute today than ever, in the era of the pandemic that placed increased strain on the availability of public finance. To make every dollar count for optimal development impacts, MDBs have prioritized consistency and quality of infrastructure project preparation as our shared goal. MDBs also recognize that the digitization of project preparation for quality infrastructure investment is vital to this end.

Repeatedly, the international community has called on MDBs to coordinate activities efficiently and effectively to ensure the best use of capital, in line with their respective mandates. The MDBs' joint initiative to establish the SOURCE platform is one such response to this call. The platform is also most timely as it enables a systemic transition to digitizing project preparation and data collection.

Both SOURCE and the Global Emerging Markets (GEMs) Risk Database Consortium are important elements of the ongoing work in support of the G20 Roadmap for Infrastructure as an Asset Class and the QII Principles. G20 finance ministers and central bank governors last year unanimously recognized this under Saudi Arabia's InfraTech Agenda (SOURCE, 2020).

The SOURCE globally supports public sector agencies to build pipelines of quality investment projects by acting as (i) a project and information management system; (ii) a database; and (iii) a marketplace—all at once. Well-prepared projects are also what governments need to attract private-sector financing. In financial benchmarking, the GEMs Risk Database Consortium remains the world's largest default and loss database for the emerging market business of international financial institutions (GEMs, 2024).

All of us know that project preparation is not like financing—there is no finish line that awaits and no ribbon to be cut. Rather, preparation is a steadfast and continuous commitment to enhance the development of viable proposals for well-prepared projects. Through such quality projects, we can either win or lose the race to deliver green, resilient, inclusive, and sustainable infrastructure for our planet.

Transport, cities, and disaster preparedness are vital for sustainable development in Asia. Despite its significant contribution to GDP and employment, transport poses challenges such as emissions and road accidents. Many countries in Asia lack access to adequate transport infrastructure, particularly in rural areas, hindering economic and social participation. Rising road fatalities and air pollution are ongoing concerns, but policy actions show some progress. Sustainable transport efforts are crucial to meet SDG targets and reduce emissions, with regional initiatives playing key roles in raising awareness and facilitating agreements to address these challenges.

## 6.5 Challenges and Opportunities in Asia's Transportation Sector

There are three critical initiatives we need to address—transport, cities, and disaster preparedness, particularly regarding water. The reason these are so important is that they are vital pillars for the future of Asia's sustainable development.

Transportation is an economy's circulatory system. While it provides access and mobility, it also creates opportunities for work, education, health, and social development. Unfortunately, it also often leads to greater emissions and, of course, road accidents. In the Asia–Pacific region, annual transport infrastructure investment requirements total approximately $866 billion, which is equivalent to around 3% of the region's GDP (AIIB, 2018). In terms of jobs, transport, and related industries employ over 165 million people, or about 8% of total employment (ADB, 2021i).

It is important to understand that transport-related activity in Asia is not commensurate with either population or GDP. Asia accounts for 58% of the world's population and contributes 49% to the global GDP. Yet, in terms of global passenger transport, its share is only 27%, while its freight transport share is 36% (ADB, 2023e). As the region continues to grow economically, transport infrastructure and transport services will also need to grow in tandem, if not accelerate.

Sustainable Development Goals (SDGs) 9.1 and 11.2 refer to how rural and urban populations worldwide can access transport to fully get involved with economic and social activity. In both cases, the SDG benchmark is universal access. Yet, there are currently 630 million rural people who do not have access to an all-weather road. And 470 million people live more than 500 meters from any modern public transportation (ADB, 2023e).

SDG target 3.6 aims to reduce road crash fatalities by half by 2030. Currently, road traffic accidents are the leading cause of death for people aged 15–29 worldwide (ADB, 2023e). The situation is particularly dire in the Asia–Pacific region, where 60% of global road crash fatalities are reported (Figure 6.5). Economists estimate that traffic accidents result in an annual loss of 6.4% of GDP in the region due to the high number of deaths and serious injuries (ADB, 2023e). In 2023, 28% of global road fatalities occurred in South-East Asia and 25% in the Western Pacific, higher than those in any other region (WHO, 2023).

Air pollution that comes from transport remains a considerable problem. $CO_2$ emissions from transport are rising most rapidly in Asia, where they have increased by 2.5 times compared to just a 50% rise in the rest of the world (ADB, 2023e). The contribution of transport to poor air quality is very high, with 76% of global deaths attributed to particulate matter (PM2.5) in the region, primarily caused by a mix of transport-related and industrial emissions (ADB, 2023e). However, there has been concerted policy action

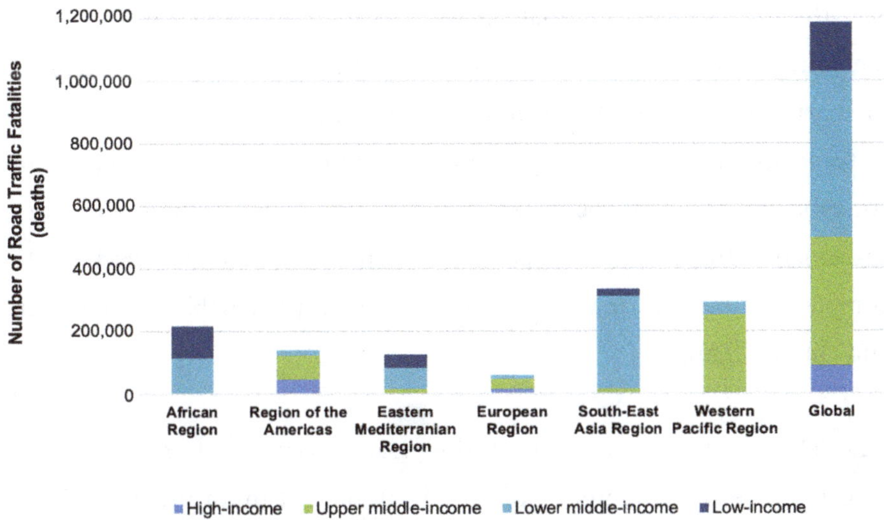


**Figure 6.5** Number of Road Traffic Fatalities in 2021
Source: Adapted from WHO (2023).

on both fuel quality and emission standards. And it has started to show results. Air quality has started to improve even as the amount of transport has increased significantly.

Unfortunately, current trends show that—in terms of emissions—transport remains one of the sectors responsible for most of the emissions increase in Asia (Asian Transport Outlook, 2023). However, we are starting to see positive developments. Business-as-usual scenarios for transport-related $CO_2$ emissions have started to change. They show a significant 50% reduction from 7 gT equivalent $CO_2$ emissions to about 4 gT by 2050 (Asian Transport Outlook, 2023).

To put it all together, we can and should expect continued growth in Asia's transportation sector. The growth in infrastructure and transport services is a prerequisite for moving forward to meet the SDG targets on transport infrastructure and access. But at the same time, it is also clear that transport should become more sustainable.

The role of regional initiatives, such as the HELP and EST (Environmentally Sustainable Transport), are important in building awareness and in sharing knowledge. We need to maximize this impact. And we need to translate new awareness and knowledge into action. One important contribution can be through regional non-legal, non-binding, voluntary agreements. These voluntary regional agreements are an important way to complement more formal global agreements on sustainable development and climate change.

> Developing Asia needs to expand its transport sector to achieve the Sustainable Development Goals (SDGs), but it cannot proceed with business as usual. The pandemic has reshaped transport across Asia, emphasizing its crucial role in development and economic growth. In the "next normal," the future of transport will involve incorporating sustainability aspects.

## 6.6 The Role of Transport in Developing Asia

These are unusual times for Asia and the world. The COVID-19 pandemic is changing the nature of transport across Asia. While the new realities of travel and transport continue to emerge and be refined, what remains constant is the role transport plays as a key enabler of development and economic growth in the region. Its fundamental role in ensuring access and mobility will not change. This is true for both in rural areas and cities—whether traveling between cities or across countries, and whether for moving people or cargo.

Transport has shown great progress in the region, with rural, national, and regional connectivity greatly improved. Access is becoming more inclusive and equitable, driving down transportation costs. Nonetheless, more investments are needed in building new infrastructure as well as for maintaining and operating existing systems.

To assess the current status of transport in developing Asia, we can use the related targets and indicators of the Sustainable Development Goals (SDGs). They can tell us how far we have come and how far we still need to go. Let us look at this from three different perspectives: first, access and connectivity; second, road safety; and third, environmental sustainability.

Transport systems need to grow to support GDP growth, fight poverty, and tackle inequality. We have seen some great improvements over recent decades. For example, today, 75% of the rural population lives within two kilometers of an all-season road (Asian Transport Outlook, 2022b). But that still means 25%—or one in four—can face problems accessing education and healthcare facilities, not to mention markets or other economic opportunities. Let me highlight a few examples of the direct link between transport infrastructure and services in Asia and the way people or countries can improve their livelihoods or economies (Rapsomanikis, 2015):

- With poor rural access, Asia's farmers have a hard time getting their produce to markets;
- Rural and urban families both find it difficult to access health and education services, or spend far too much time getting to work;
- Poor connectivity between transport systems in Asia—nationally and regionally—is a nontariff barrier to economic integration.

The work done to address these issues has been quite remarkable. To maintain these trends, we must continue to provide new infrastructure as well as ensure there are adequate budgets for maintenance. There is also the urgent need to continue connecting rural and urban transport services. Hundreds of millions of people will rely on this increased connectivity, which is essential if we are to continue an upward trajectory toward meeting SDG targets.

The second aspect is road safety. In Asia and the Pacific, the number of people killed or severely injured in traffic accidents is alarmingly high. Annually, approximately 800,000 individuals lose their lives in road crashes, which results in economic costs of about $1 trillion (Asian Transport Outlook, 2022a).

Tackling road safety is fundamental to achieving the SDGs, specifically those affecting health security, sustainable cities, and reducing inequality among countries. Action is needed across all sectors to reduce the mortality and morbidity from road accidents.

While transport offers many development opportunities, it also brings several negative externalities—particularly in terms of environmental and climate impact. The sector still increasingly relies on fossil fuels, and its emissions contribute to poor air quality and increased carbon dioxide, or $CO_2$ (Figure 6.6). This is the third perspective of environment sustainability.

How do we address transport's environmental and climate impact as the region continues to grow and develop? Fuel subsidies should be carefully considered to promote more equitable and sustainable modes of transportation. Fuel quality and travel options, especially within our cities, must be urgently addressed to improve local air quality and the dramatic impact it has on human health. We must also address the increasing levels of $CO_2$ produced and continue to prioritize a more balanced multimodal transport system—one that promotes energy efficiency and reduces emissions (ADB, 2023e).

This quick assessment on SDG targets clearly shows that developing Asia will need to expand its transport sector to meet SDG targets on social and economic development. Yet it also shows and underscores the fact that we cannot achieve this development in a business-as-usual manner.

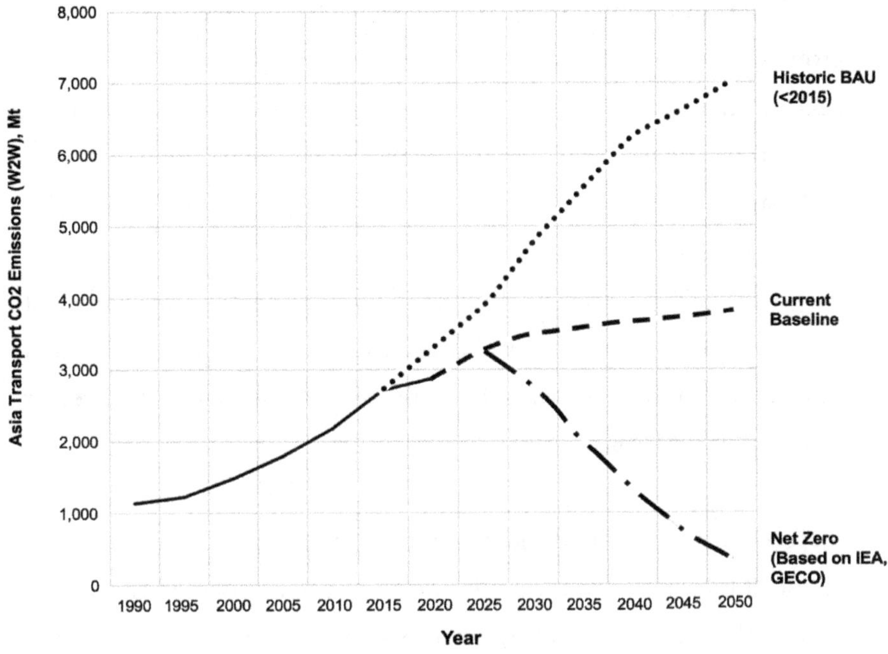


**Figure 6.6** Transport Business-as-Usual Emissions in the Asia–Pacific
Source: Adapted from Asian Transport Outlook (2022a).

A good idea would be to develop a regional transport scorecard that measures the sector's performance against international agreements and commitments. The scorecard will allow a greater understanding of key issues, enhance both dialogue and the decision-making process to deliver a more sustainable transport future. In the process, it will strengthen regional approaches for the sector.

I would like to share three recent examples of transport projects. They exemplify ways of combining transport sector growth with increased sustainability—which will be the future of transport in the "next normal":

- First is the Karachi Bus Rapid Transit Red Line Project in Pakistan. The Bus Rapid Transit (BRT) will help improve urban access through bus-based public transport. It will relieve congestion, minimize road accidents, and reduce the pollution that would have come from the growing use of private cars.

- Second, the Mumbai Metro Rail Systems Project in India will help develop two lines for the Mumbai Metro Rail System. This will ease the daily stress on millions of commuters and help provide a cleaner, less congested city.
- Last is the EDSA Greenway Project in the Philippines. This will create five kilometers of elevated walkways to provide safe access to public transit and improve the walkability of some of the main urban centers across Metro-Manila.

Before closing, I would like to briefly come back to the COVID-19 pandemic. It is clear the pandemic is posing an unprecedented challenge—not just to the transport sector, but to the overall economic and social development of the entire region.

But we will also continue to prepare for the period after COVID-19. In the case of Asia, this means planning for a larger—and more sustainable—transport sector. The future role of transport in developing Asia requires strengthening the regional approach. I believe that regional events are pivotal in moving common objectives forward. By learning from each other's knowledge and experience, we can work together to shape the next normal of Asia's sustainable transport.

Toward the end of the pandemic's first year, while the immediate responses were primarily domestic; when it came to trade and transportation, it was clear greater regional cooperation would be needed to reduce barriers to trade and ease regional connectivity.

## 6.7 Impact of COVID-19 on Global Trade and Transport

As you all know, the pandemic has sent shockwaves across the global economy and trade. It slashed the volume of world merchandise trade by 8% year-on-year for the first eight months of 2020. The World Trade Organization forecasts that the overall trade volume will fall by 9% in 2020. Although it should rebound by about 7% in 2021, this is still well below the pre-crisis levels (WTO, 2020). To make things worse, even these estimates could be over-optimistic, depending on a variety of factors, including:

(i)   Whether new outbreaks can be avoided;

(ii)  Whether governments will be forced to impose additional lockdowns; and

(iii) Whether pent-up demand will be exhausted.

The pandemic exposed many weaknesses in transport and trade. Among them is the region's high dependence on paper-based documentation in trade transactions.

Asia and the Pacific region has done well in facilitating general trade measures over the past decades. However, it has lagged in digital trade facilitation (UN, 2021). The pandemic has made clear that there remain gaps in the automation of document clearance, subregional coordination, and implementation of emergency protocols—nationally and regionally. The outbreak also created more barriers to accessing trade finance. This is a persistent obstacle for the small and medium enterprises in particular.

COVID-19 had also a devastating impact across the transport sector. Travel restrictions since the outbreak continue in many places—although several "corridors" between hubs may open soon. Nonetheless, after tourism and hospitality, the transport sector was the hardest hit by the pandemic. An estimated 17% of households in the region depend on income from the transport industry (ADB, 2020a). This means that transport restrictions and disruptions to international trade are causing serious economic hardship for the millions of people who work in the sector.

The International Transport Forum estimates that global freight volumes in 2020 are likely to fall by more than one-third (International Transport Forum, 2020). In March 2020, the aviation subsector alone saw a 28% reduction in capacity in Asia and the Pacific, compared to March 2019 (ADB, 2020a). Air cargo services essential for transporting high-value commodities have been hit hard. This is especially difficult for the more remote Pacific Island countries that rely heavily on aviation for supplies and tourism. Flight schedule disruptions are commonplace in developing countries throughout the region. Shipping has also been deeply affected by enhanced quarantine requirements and handling disruptions at ports—a subsector that carries the bulk of international cargo.

Infrastructure, along with the logistics and technology it provides, is the lifeline of regional trade. Let me offer some examples of regional transport connectivity projects.

Central Asia has developed multi-modal transport corridors as part of the Central Asia Regional Economic Cooperation (CAREC) program (ADB, 2020a). The CAREC Transport Strategy, released in January this year, sets out ways for countries to further collaborate on completing missing links in the corridor and enhancing regional transport services.

Efforts are also being made to incorporate more local facilities into the logistics chain. In June 2020, a report titled "Developing Multimodal Logistics Parks in India" was produced by ADB, and proposals for the Phnom Penh Logistics Complex were prepared. By integrating local facilities into international corridors with greater connectivity, improvements in corridor efficiency will be achieved, transportation costs will be reduced, and the increasing demand for shipping freight will be satisfied.

What do we need to do differently in the post COVID-19 environment?

More investment in resilient connectivity—by improving health infrastructure, protocols, and facilities at entry gateways, ports, and airports—can be beneficial. A good example is the Sri Lanka Health System Enhancement Project (HSEP, 2022). The project will strengthen health information systems and disease surveillance capacity as well as implementation of international health regulation standards in critical ports of entry.

Clearly, the pandemic strained budgets in many developing countries in the region. As such, we need to use existing subregional platforms and investments to attract the private sector to join high-quality, green infrastructure projects (ADB, 2020a). It is also essential to narrow the persistently wide connectivity gap across Asia and the Pacific. With this in mind, the ASEAN Catalytic Green Finance Facility was established (ADB, 2022i). This infrastructure fund assists governments in Southeast Asia prepare and finance infrastructure projects that draw in private sector infrastructure investment; promote environmental sustainability; and help reach climate change goals.

One thing the pandemic response made clear is that digitalization will play an increasingly critical role in the post-pandemic "next normal." I believe digitalization will enhance the resilience of the global production system and supply chains, thereby helping foster new drivers of economic growth. Let me expand a bit more on this.

Before COVID-19 struck, digitalization of supply chains was already improving operation efficiency. Post-pandemic, countries need to significantly boost investment to expand digitalization capabilities in both public and private sectors. Importantly, countries will have to ensure it is coordinated regionally for interoperability, data security, and harmonized protocols.

Trade facilitation measures will also need to embrace digitalization more deeply. Regional dialogue can do a lot to ensure cross-country information exchange and acceptance of digital certificates done through properly secured systems.

For example, trade facilitation initiatives under the South Asia Subregional Economic Cooperation Program, or SASEC, seeks to modernize and advance cross-border e-commerce by streamlining legal frameworks, customs processes, and the use of information and communications technology (SASEC, 2017).

Finally, regional cooperation can play an important role in reducing shared health risks. Governments need to cooperate to harmonize health and safety protocols so that critical connectivity infrastructure—such as ports and airports—remain open during crises.

The unprecedented health and economic crisis has heightened the urgency for facilitating trade and transport for sustainable development.

There are many indications of how economies in Asia and the Pacific continue to work toward free trade and the multilateral trade system. The latest of such collective effort was the signing of the Regional Comprehensive Economic Partnership agreement by 15 economies on 15 November 2020 (ASEAN, 2023c). The agreement underscores the Asian and Pacific leaders' commitment to deepen regional cooperation and boost free trade for the greater prosperity of the region.

Chapter **7**

**Sustainable Development Goals
(The SDGs, gender and youth)**

## 7.1 Introduction

The 17 United Nations worldwide Sustainable Development Goals (SDGs) run from 2016 to 2030 (with 169 targets and 231 unique indicators). To say the least, they are ambitious. Yet they provide a very important global direction for development, whether economic or social. They are the next step (some call it a reboot) of the 8 groundbreaking Millennium Development Goals (21 targets and 63 indicators), which applied to emerging economies from 2000 to 2015.

While supported by nearly all countries in Asia and the Pacific, achieving them is a definitely worthy if massive undertaking. They cover eradicating poverty and hunger to ensuring health, education, good jobs, and gender equality. They deal with energy, infrastructure, and climate change, among others.

Prior to the pandemic all were below their 2020 targets. COVID-19 threw an anvil into the works, as budgets and financing were channeled to immediate needs. Two years later, however, recovery plans began integrating the SDGs into their overall direction. Many understood that to make them work, they needed to move forward in providing far greater social protection within a localized, community context. Within developing Asia and the Pacific, ensuring gender equality and absorbing the large number of young people in many economies stand out as ways to grow more equitably and inclusively.

The chapter covers all these and ways to better move toward achieving the SDG targets. Mobilizing multilateral, public, and private financing to move the SDG process forward is a primary challenge.

The pandemic invigorated two approaches that could drive progress on the SDGs: the first on localizing the SDG agenda, particularly in cities; the second on financing, in particular new ways to attract private investment to support SDG targets.

## 7.2 Innovation to Implement the SDGs in Asia and the Pacific

The pandemic's toll has been immense, setting back progress in a region that was already off track to meet the SDGs. Yet, while the COVID-19 disrupted all of our lives, it has also shown the capacity of the Asia and the Pacific region to innovate and reinvent. We have found new ways to work, to do business, and communicate.

Governments have worked hard to contain the spread of COVID-19 while continuing to deliver essential services. Unprecedented government, private sector, and multilateral collaboration largely succeeded in accessing and distributing the vaccines that will lead out of this human and economic crisis and back on the road to recovery. While the pandemic is far from over, it has shown our capacity to take on difficult problems by using science, technology, finance, and partnerships.

The pandemic reinforced the importance of integrating the SDG agenda. There are costs of failing to address seemingly unconnected issues as a whole. The SDGs were designed to address the very gaps and weaknesses the pandemic exposed. And while the future may look uncertain, the pandemic also hit the "fast forward" button on the critical factors that can accelerate progress on the SDGs. However, progress on the SDGs in Asia and the Pacific has been uneven, with some areas regressing and others advancing at a slow pace (Figure 7.1).

Innovation that engages all levels and actors in society is key. Let me start first with localization as a transformative approach for accelerating the implementation of the SDGs. Cities will likely be the hubs of innovation that will offer new solutions to stubborn challenges.

Localization is critical for creating an integrated framework for SDG policymaking and delivery by subnational governments (Global Taskforce of Local and Regional Governments, 2016). Subnational institutions are critically important for recovery. The pandemic showed how important public institutions are in their capacity to provide services for all, and in particular the most vulnerable in our society. Governments relied on existing public institutions and service delivery mechanisms for health services to enforce containment measures and to provide social and economic relief. At the same time, however, it also underscored the existing weaknesses and fragilities of public sector systems. It was the subnational governments—in particular cities—that were at the frontlines in containing the pandemic, distributing relief, and currently getting vaccines into people's arms equitably.

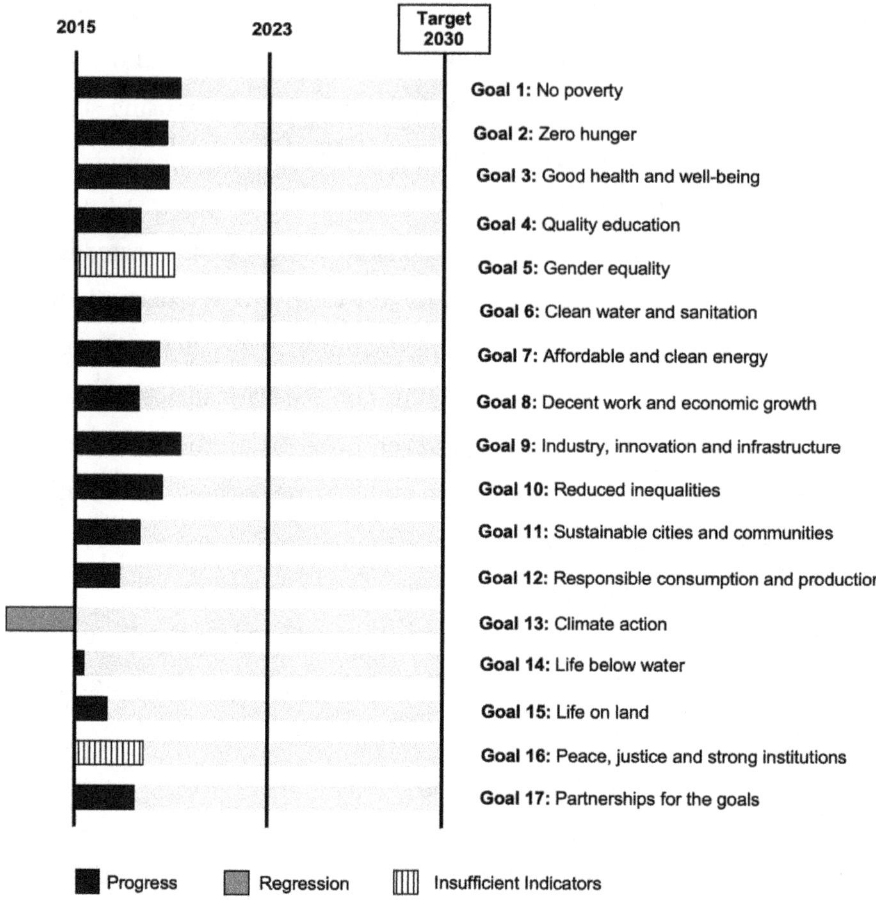


**Figure 7.1** Progress on the SDGs in Asia and the Pacific
Source: Adapted from UNESCAP (2024).

The pandemic raises the question of whether the existing distribution of responsibilities and resources between levels of government allows us to deal with high-impact shocks, such as a global health crisis. There needs to be more effective coordination between various tiers of government. This has never been more clear. And it has been a topic at meetings including those of the development working group of the G20.

Let me turn to how to measure SDG impact.

We all know that meeting the SDGs requires immense financing. And the pandemic has made this even more difficult. Financing for the SDGs requires steering all possible forms of capital toward attaining these goals (MDBs and IMF, 2020).

The growing focus on impact measurement and standards that reflect the SDGs among public and private investors gives us optimism. However, much more remains to be done to ensure these standards are coherent, ambitious, and feasible. We will discuss this at tomorrow's SDG Dialogue.

Localizing the SDGs and creating impact standards are two frontiers for accelerating progress toward meeting the SDGs.

As mentioned, localization means shifting the focus from traditional centrally led SDG implementation to subnational entities, such as cities and regions. The push to develop standards to measure and align investments with the SDGs, on the other hand, gives a sharper focus to the longstanding effort to integrate environmental, social, and governance into mainstream investment.

The greater focus on impact investment also widens subnational and urban investment opportunities. That allows forward-looking cities and regions to find new ways to attract a range of investors to help meet their financing needs for sustainable, green, inclusive, and resilient development. This all helps better align public and private approaches for the SDGs at all levels of government and across all parts of the economy.

As the previous speech explained, localizing the SDGs gives ownership on the ground. This speech delves deeper into the institutional reforms necessary to facilitate the process, focusing on the optimal approach to decentralization for effectively achieving SDG targets.

## 7.3 Localizing the Sustainable Development Goals

The "Decade of Action," announced in September 2019, calls for accelerating sustainable solutions to challenges ranging from poverty and gender to climate change, inequality and closing the finance gap (UN, 2020). This ambitious worldwide effort works on three levels: globally, locally, and at the personal level. It remains to be the global roadmap for sustainable and inclusive development. And amid this pandemic, the SDGs are more relevant than ever and provide the very framework for recovery.

The devastating impact of the pandemic is leaving some deep scars in Asia and the Pacific region's growth and development. Estimated economic losses worldwide reached $4.8 trillion to $7.4 trillion in 2020, with developing Asia accounting for about 28% of the total. And by the end of 2020, some 78 million more people had found themselves below the $1.90-a-day poverty line (ADB, 2020b).

It is clear that we must move urgently to pursue more sustainable and inclusive development strategies that allow communities to weather these kinds of shocks.

What will the recovery from the COVID-19 look like?

Some economists are hoping for a quick, V-shaped recovery, while others have warned of a slower, U-shaped rebound. Today, yet another possibility is emerging—that of a K-shaped recovery. The "K-shaped" recovery is characterized by a stark split in the recovery pace of the economy—some sectors are bouncing back ahead of the rest at a much faster pace, while others are continuing a downward trajectory. This split in the recovery pace, therefore, resembles the letter "K."

The pandemic is also threatening to deepen the divide between developed and developing countries and cause greater economic divergence within the countries in the region, in part as a result of inequitable digitalization. Sectors that strategically and effectively adopt digital initiatives will likely see their profits pointing upward. Online inter-activities through mobile apps or websites are occupying more space in our daily life in this age of social distancing and COVID-19 measures. Companies that are able to meet their customers' needs through digital services will likely reap the benefits from both increased patronage and cost savings.

Meanwhile, developing countries, smaller businesses, and poorer communities have had more difficulties adapting to the dramatic and transformative digital leap that has been witnessed since the pandemic. But harnessing digitalization, expanding access to technology, and improving digital literacy will all be critical for avoiding the K-shaped recovery.

Localizing the SDGs is another important and crucial prerequisite for a successful pandemic recovery—and for returning to a path capable of achieving the SDGs. About two-thirds of the 169 SDG targets involve subnational governments (Sachs *et al.*, 2019).

They also account for nearly a quarter of total public spending and more than a third of public investment. Education, social protection, health, and other public services are the primary areas of subnational government spending that link closely with the SDGs (OECD and UCLG, 2019).

Localization is critically important in Asia and the Pacific. The megatrends of rapid urbanization, climate response, population growth, and demographic change are just some of the challenges. Last year, we saw the importance of subnational and local governments in containing the spread of COVID-19, getting relief to those in need, and keeping essential services functioning. Yet, we need a better enabling environment that allows subnational governments to better contribute to national SDG agendas.

This involves four key elements: (i) strengthening institutions and policy coherence across government; (ii) finance; (iii) keeping tabs on what is happening through effective data collection and monitoring; and (iv) ensuring we engage with all stakeholders, develop partnerships, and share knowledge (UNDP, 2021).

Let me briefly expand on these four elements.

We must strengthen institutions and ensure coherent policies. A 2019 report by United Cities and Local Governments found that despite efforts to clarify the allocation of responsibilities, there remain significant overlaps between different levels of government in many countries in Asia and the Pacific (UCLG, 2019a).

Much remains to be done to help developing countries align the legal, institutional, and fiscal dimensions of their decentralization frameworks, while at the same time reduce constraints on building technical and management capacity.

Second, subnational government finance must be robust, sustainable, and predictable. Mobilizing financing remains a major challenge. Debt risk was already rising in many developing countries prior to the pandemic. The fiscal stimulus response was appropriate but exacerbated the state of those with high debt and low revenue. Several developing Asian countries do not meet the threshold 15% of GDP tax yield—which is now widely regarded as the minimum required for sustainable development. Developing countries in Asia and the Pacific must urgently expand their tax base.

Increasing domestic resource mobilization should be a priority. Tax system reforms and enforcement, as well as more equitable intergovernmental fiscal transfer systems can be options. Initiatives like the Asia–Pacific Tax Hub are examples that can strengthen mobilization and facilitate international tax cooperation among countries, in collaboration with other development partners.

This requires an attractive investment climate within an appropriate regulatory framework and effective government oversight. Standards on the quality, inclusiveness, and reliability of services are needed to ensure safety, as well as social and environmental protection (UNCTAD, 2014).

Innovative financing mechanisms are essential, like how philanthropic organizations can play an increasingly prominent role in supporting the SDGs.

Third, we must combine different approaches to better track progress on SDGs. On the one hand, we must not forget that public statistics systems will remain key. On the other hand, far more granular data at the subnational levels can be gathered through community-based approaches. In Asia and the Pacific, many countries have made huge strides in the past few years to improve the quality and quantity of national-level data, particularly creating gender-disaggregated data sets and more precise subnational information. To support this trend, a Data for Development initiative was established to build more granular data that are relevant to the SDGs and working closely with the National Statistical Offices.

Finally, to ensure that "no one is left behind," we must further expand and deepen partnerships among all stakeholders at all levels, both within and outside the country. Civil society, academia, and the private sector all play critical roles in accelerating SDG implementation. With financing needs too large to be shouldered by the public sector alone, private sector partnerships will only grow in importance.

We are beginning to see more evidence that localized approach to SDGs is an effective strategy. The United Cities and Local Governments report in 2019, for example, has argued that the systematic sharing of knowledge and lessons learned among countries hold considerable potentials to accelerate localized SDG initiatives (UCLG, 2019b).

More than one year on, we know that the pandemic has most likely worsened Asia and the Pacific countries' prospects of meeting their SDG targets. The challenges have become greater and urgent actions are on call.

But there is cause for optimism too. Let us remind ourselves how in the past year, thanks to the global partnerships and collaboration, the world has made unprecedented progress in development, production, and dissemination of the COVID-19 vaccines—not just one but several.

> The innovative "graduation approach" can be done to remove poverty and reduce inequality, thus promoting economic opportunities and social inclusion. The poor and vulnerable can benefit from this approach by receiving a big push toward sustainable livelihoods and resilience, leading to a better future.

## 7.4 Social Protection for Economic Inclusion 2021

Social Protection for Economic Inclusion explains how we use "the graduation approach" to reduce poverty in Asia and the Pacific. It is all about graduating out of poverty with the ability to create sustainable livelihoods.

As you all know, Asia and the Pacific made considerable progress in development and poverty reduction over the past 50 years. Yet, even before the pandemic, the region was still home to nearly 264 million people living in extreme poverty ($1.90/day)—and 836 million living on less than $3.20/day (ADB, 2018).

The COVID-19 pandemic significantly disrupted life across much of Asia and the Pacific. It set back economies in terms of poverty, inequality, and employment. And it exacerbated pre-existing vulnerabilities for some groups. In fact, an estimation by ADB shows that 78 million people may have been added to the ranks of those considered extremely poor (ADB, 2020c).

Those disproportionately affected include children, youth, women, informal workers, the elderly, and people with disabilities.

The truth is that over 60% of the region's population was not covered by adequate social protection prior to the pandemic (ADB, 2021j). And as the crisis has merely underscored, social protection is vital to safeguard and protect those most vulnerable to poverty.

It is clearer than ever that we must strengthen social protection systems and adopt innovative approaches that recognize the multidimensional nature of poverty. What we call the graduation approach is one such innovation. It is built on a foundation of social assistance and enables households to achieve socioeconomic resilience.

Graduation programs deliver a carefully sequenced set of integrated solutions to poor households, combining social assistance with asset transfers, livelihood promotion, financial inclusion, and social empowerment, along with dedicated mentoring and coaching (Figure 7.2; ADB, 2023f). Together, when adapted to local contexts, these graduation approach pillars help lead to long-term, sustainable, and resilient livelihoods—with measurable improvements in people's lives.

We believe graduation programs can offer governments a promising pathway to meet the needs of people currently living in poverty. And it builds resilience against potential shocks.

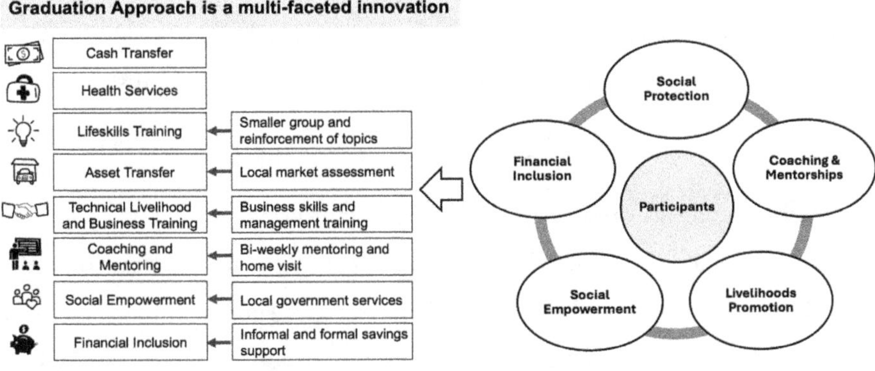


**Figure 7.2** Graduation Approach
Source: Adapted from ADB (2023f).

One example is the first pilot use of the graduation approach in the Philippines, which is contributing to an increasing amount of compelling global evidence. The pilot took place in the province of Negros Occidental and concluded in 2020 (ADB, 2021k). The Department of Labor and Employment (DOLE) led implementation with support from civil society partners—Building Resources Across Communities and Innovations for Poverty Action.

The pilot project targeted 1,800 poor households, building on the government's existing, but separate, cash transfer and livelihood programs. It tested several ways of delivering elements of the graduation approach to individuals and groups. The results were then compared with a group of households that only received the cash transfers. A preliminary analysis of the September 2020 mobile phone survey showed that the graduation approach improved household resilience against the COVID-19 shock in several ways—including financial health, food security, and mental health.

In addition, there are now three additional graduation programs:

- for resettled households in the Philippines under the Malolos-Clark Railway Project;
- in Tamil Nadu, India as part of the Inclusive, Resilient and Sustainable Housing for Urban Poor Sector Project; and finally
- in Mongolia as part of the Second Shock-Responsive Social Protection Project.

Ensuring gender equality is one of the main goals of SDGs. United Nations Women's advocacy has helped policymakers focus attention on gender equality as a vital means of achieving these goals. The following speech emphasizes the need for collective and urgent actions to address gender-related challenges exacerbated by the COVID-19 pandemic.

## 7.5 Promoting Gender Equality in COVID-19 Response and Recovery

Collective and urgent actions are needed to find sustainable solutions to the many gender-related COVID-19 challenges. We heard about the difficulties faced by women and girls, as many lost employment and livelihoods. Their reduced access to key services, including maternal healthcare, has also been acute. In today's discussions, we also learned about the urgency to collect reliable gender data to better track COVID-19's gender impacts.

Above all, the discussions revisited the importance of stepping up support to developing countries in their quest to achieve the ambitious vision of SDG 5 on gender equality.

In 2018, there was a study titled, Gender Equality and the SDGs in Asia and the Pacific, by ADB and UN Women. The study made an important contribution of looking at gender data gaps in the SDG framework in Asia and the Pacific (ADB and UN Women, 2018).

Several other initiatives related to gender equality at the country level include:

- gender-responsive budgeting in India and Viet Nam;
- gender country assessments in Myanmar and the Kyrgyz Republic; and
- workshops on solutions to gender-based violence in several Central and West Asian countries.

With the COVID-19 and its threats to gender equality gains in the region, collaboration between stakeholders is essential in the following four priority areas:

1. Enhanced technical collaboration on SDG 5, aiming to strengthen data and evidence on gender-related SDGs. This will contribute

significantly to the region, particularly in assessing COVID-19 impacts on SDG progress and improving the availability of sex-disaggregated data, crucial for informing COVID-19 response and monitoring government programs.

2. Promotion of gender-responsive budgeting as a governance tool in response to COVID-19. Gender-responsive budgeting can enhance efficiency in public resource spending and safeguard earmarked resources for gender equality. Collaboration will involve building awareness and technical capacity of developing countries on gender-responsive budgeting, essential for better monitoring of how COVID-19 stimulus programs support women and girls.

3. Promotion of gender-responsive procurement to support women's businesses and jobs. The COVID-19 pandemic poses a significant threat to women-owned businesses and jobs, necessitating action to expand market opportunities for them. A joint research initiative can be launched to facilitate access to markets for women-owned or women-led businesses.

4. Development of a comprehensive response to tackle gender-based violence, which has escalated as a destructive consequence of the COVID-19 pandemic. Collaboration will involve stepped-up data collection, community outreach campaigns, and specialized training for healthcare workers to identify and treat victims.

One of the challenges related to gender equality imposed by the pandemic is the disproportionate impact on women as they struggled to keep their jobs and families functioning. The following section provides some takeaways from the Gender Forum, highlighting the importance of gender equality for achieving inclusive and sustainable development.

## 7.6 The Power to Transform: Gender Equality in Asia and the Pacific

The pandemic reminds us that progress on gender equality cannot be taken for granted. Women are more vulnerable to pandemic-related impacts because of existing gender inequality. These effects are more evident in the Asia–Pacific region due to pre-existing cultural biases on gender and various social norms that make women and girls particularly vulnerable.

Now, we are collectively and urgently tackling both the pandemic recovery and the climate crisis. We must "build forward better" for a more gender-equal and resilient world. The recent ADB Gender Forum in 2021 offered valuable insights and takeaways that underscored the urgency of this mission.

Anu Madgavkar's exploration of the potential long-term effects of COVID-19 on the workforce highlighted the need for countries to adapt and support women in a rapidly evolving job market. As economies transition toward net zero emissions, Madgavkar emphasized the emergence of new opportunities for women, particularly in areas such as remote work, digital transactions, and automation. However, critical issues around the impact of automation on the labor market, especially for women, were also raised. Unpaid care work, often performed by women, remains excluded from formal economic definitions, underscoring the importance of addressing societal norms and investing in the care economy to ensure women's full participation in the workforce.

The key messages are that we need to continue to invest in the care economy, address social and gender norms, support women's access to modern knowledge and skills so they can be an active part of the changing economy. We need to look at new sectors as essential generators of jobs for women.

In the realm of urban development, Maria Vassilakou offered insights into how cities of the future can be designed to better meet the needs of women and girls. Drawing from examples in Vienna, Vassilakou highlighted the importance of gender mainstreaming in city planning and the need for inclusive design practices. Panel discussions further emphasized the necessity of gender-sensitive infrastructure planning, advocating for gender-based analysis of space and decision-making processes that actively involve women and girls in city planning endeavors.

Turning toward climate action, Sharan Burrow of the International Trade Union Confederation emphasized the role of women in driving transformative change toward a greener, more equitable future. Burrow challenged participants to rethink notions of decent work and underscored the importance of supporting women-led climate action initiatives. Panelists echoed these sentiments, stressing the crucial role women play in climate change mitigation and adaptation efforts. However, it was also recognized that women often face disproportionate risks and vulnerabilities in the face of climate change, highlighting the need for targeted support and investment in women's resilience-building efforts.

In addition to discussions on climate action, the forum also addressed the pervasive issue of gender-based violence and the importance of prioritizing the informal economy. Guest speakers such as Imrana Jalal and Padma Shri Reema Nanavati offered valuable insights into the prevalence and impact of gender-based violence, as well as the need to prioritize the informal economy and grassroots women's movements in discussions on gender equality and women's empowerment.

In summary, the ADB Gender Forum in 2021 served as a catalyst for meaningful dialogue and action toward advancing gender equality and women's empowerment across the Asia–Pacific region. As we continue to navigate the complex intersections of gender, climate, and economic challenges, it is imperative that we heed the lessons and insights gleaned from this forum to build a more inclusive and resilient future for all.

This speech, relatively early into the pandemic, describes how people viewed the challenges expected as the battle against COVID-19 intensified. Education and training play crucial roles in addressing the challenges, such as urbanization and climate change for a sustainable future.

## 7.7 Future of Education, Sustainable Cities, and the SDGs

We are today at significant crossroads in the path toward inclusive and sustainable development of Asia and the Pacific. Against this background, I would like to discuss what initial observations and lessons can be drawn from the COVID-19 and the "new normal"; what they mean for the region's development challenges; and why education and skills development hold one of the important keys to meeting these challenges, particularly in the context of urbanization.

I would first like to draw your attention to the five drivers of change, which have increasingly been shaping the world. The success of efforts to combat the effects of the pandemic will, in part, hinge on how well we can leverage these drivers to our advantage:

(i) First, the ripples of *technologies* continue to influence almost all parts of our life—some of them helpful, while others disruptive. We do not need to look further for examples than new technology's effects on the mode of education, as well as job creation or destruction. Reading the widely available literature on these subjects, I remain optimistic that we can leverage technology effectively to equip more people with the skills needed in the future, and to provide more learning opportunities to all members of our societies.

(ii) Second, we have been witnessing *rapid urbanization* across the world and particularly in Asia and the Pacific. The share of people living in cities in Asia and the Pacific Region has increased from 20% in the 1950s to 48% in 2018. This is expected to increase to 55% by 2030, which translates to 2.5 billion people (ADB, 2019d). Throughout this transformation, cities have driven growth, acted as the main vehicle for poverty reduction, and served as the cradle of innovation. They will continue to do so in the future, which means that our efforts to address the challenges of skills development are closely tied to those for building sustainable and smart cities.

(iii) Third, *climate change* has the potential to derail our hard-earned improvements. Greenhouse gas (GHG) emissions from the region have risen rapidly, from 25% of the global total in the 1990s to 40% in 2012. This could reach nearly 50% by 2030, of which, cities are responsible for generating about 75% (ADB, 2019d). Cities in the region are indeed suffering from increasing vehicular emissions and unmanaged solid waste disposal, which aggravate the global carbon footprint. We could, therefore, say that managing sustainable development of cities holds the key to reversing our overall carbon footprint.

(iv) Fourth, people continue to look for new opportunities outside of their immediate localities, many moving as far away as to other countries. While *all* countries are affected by *labor mobility* within the national boundaries or beyond, *some* economies are more dependent on remittances than others. It is noteworthy that the ASEAN region recognizes this ever-growing phenomenon and is collaborating in promoting mutual recognition of education and skills certifications.

This is an area where fruitful collaboration and partnership will be high on the future agenda to facilitate more mobility.

(v)  The fifth and final driver is *demographic changes.* On one hand, some countries in Asia, like the People's Republic of China, Thailand and Sri Lanka, are already aging necessitating people to have a prolonged working life. They are facing the need to increase productivity to do more with fewer people at work and to innovate continuously to help older people work for longer years. On the other hand, there are many other countries that still have young population with potential for demographic dividends. In both scenarios, more investments are needed in human capital to optimize returns.

We all agree that the COVID-19 pandemic is a wake-up call for all of us. The five drivers of change will help us tackle the question of how we can turn this crisis into an opportunity to address and redress existing challenges and to reimagine a new normal. Let me share four lessons:

(i)  First, we have seen dramatic improvements in air quality in some of the most polluted cities in Asia and the Pacific region. As a result, many diseases related to air pollution such as asthma and other respiratory ailments have subsided. As governments begin to re-open the economy, we must ensure that their policies and development work come together to improve the natural environment as well.

(ii)  Second, the sudden closure of schools has forced education systems to shift to online learning. While *none of us* were ready for a disruption of this magnitude, the effects of the pandemic have not been equitable. In fact, students who are suffering the most are the ones with limited means from poorer households. They have taken a higher share of those lagging behind in learning, and they are at a higher risk of being left behind further, due to the uneven or unavailable internet connectivity. How can we ensure *learning for all* in the era of pandemic? It is high time we took multifaceted approaches of using advance technology and strategic investments in critical areas such as connectivity, digital contents, teacher readiness, and support to parents.

(iii)  Third, many in the workforce have lost their jobs with no immediate prospect for regaining them. Increased competition and changing job market demands mean that, more than ever, reskilling and upskilling have become pressing needs. The pandemic has triggered a sudden rise in the demand for skills on certain professions, as well as a sharp decline in others. The immediate increase was recorded in health work, e-commerce, logistics, and public works, among others, but more dramatic changes in the job markets could well be on their way. We must continuously innovate to support the skill development to help people cope with these changes, especially among the vulnerable social groups.

(iv)  This leads to the fourth and last point on social protection. We are facing a high risk that COVID-19 could reverse the region's hard-gained poverty reduction achievements. Now is the time to find innovative ways to protect the most vulnerable through social assistance programs, in partnership with employers, private sector, and education and training institutions.

Asia and the Pacific has remarkable track record on economic growth, as reflected in the term, *Asian Century,* coined for the 21st century. While the so-called tiger economies[1] have led this performance, many

---

[1] Republic of Korea, Singapore, Hong Kong, China and Taipei, China.

developing countries in the region are also growing at impressive rates to reach a middle-income level. Their key priorities are threefold:

(i) First, they want to avoid the middle-income trap. If the current momentum of growth continues across the region—true to the *Asian Century* scenario—the projection shows that the GDP could reach $148 trillion by 2050. But under the middle-income trap scenario, it could stall at as low as $61 trillion (ADB, 2011b). This is where I bring your attention to the importance of sustainable development, as enshrined in the global SDGs. Countries are aware that, for the *Asian Century* scenario to happen, investments cannot be focused on infrastructure only. Rather, they must be balanced with human capital development, retooling of institutions for good governance, and many other aspects of sustainable development.

(ii) Second, with high growth in Asia and the Pacific region, inequality is also rising in many countries. To ensure everyone is able to achieve their full potential, it will be important to take a lifecycle approach of investing in people from an early stage and sustaining that investment. What the tiger economies have demonstrated is that such inclusive human capital development approach must be blended well with other policies, including industrial policy and innovation strategy. The tiger economies have also shown that many of their urban centers have provided greater opportunities to the inhabitants through public–private partnerships and smart city development strategies.

(iii) Third, the hard-earned development is threatened by the impacts of climate change and its associated costs. Once again, I come back to the SDGs, how we must all do our part to fast track the achievements of the 17 goals to create a resilient and sustainable society.

Ultimately, we must adopt a people-centered development to make everyone happy and responsive.

I would like to highlight two specific challenges faced by developing countries in education and training sectors. First is despite impressive improvements in access to education at all levels, a significant portion of the population in many countries is not learning at the desired pace or level. In other words, the school attendance rate may have increased, but many students are not able to demonstrate the required competency when finishing schools. This is known as the "leaning crisis." The second related point is that, despite the graduates' improved education and training, some employers are unable to fill vacancies. This is because the graduates do not meet the employers' skills requirements, and the graduates, in turn, are unable to find jobs which match their qualifications.

What does this mean for the future of education and training in Asia and the Pacific? The lifecycle approach of improving foundational literacy and numeracy from an early stage must be complemented with lifelong learning of digital skills and soft skills (Figure 7.3).[2] The old ways of relying on narrowly defined occupational skills are no longer an option.

New generation technologies, such as adaptive learning and labor market tools, are providing fresh opportunities to scale up quality and to reduce skills mismatches. On the school side, adaptive learning is helping teachers to understand which students are lagging behind and in what domains. The data generated by adaptive learning technologies help teachers and researchers to develop remedial measures that students can use to personalize their learning and sustain improvements at their own pace. Similarly, AI tools can generate data from professional job portals to

---

[2]Soft skills include: Leadership skills, teamwork, communication skills, creativity, problem solving skills, work ethic, flexibility/adaptability, time management, and interpersonal skills.

## Learning for all

**Two major challenges**
- Learning crisis
- Skills mismatches

**Foundational skills**
- Literacy and numeracy
- Digital skills
- Soft skills

**Occupational skills**
- Common skills
- Sector specific skills
- Vertical and horizontal mobility: reskilling and upskilling

**Role of technology**
- Adaptive and personalized learning
- Labor market intelligence system

**Figure 7.3** Learning for All
Source: Adapted from ADB (2022b).

identify how occupations are changing and what skills are becoming more important. This can be matched with individual skills profile to allow job seekers to sharpen their competencies in areas where they can enhance.

These challenges and opportunities for education and skills development need to be analyzed against the background of rapid urbanization, one of the five drivers of change.

There is a two-way process between urbanization and improved education and skills sector. On one hand, education can fuel the dynamism of cities and provide the human resources to drive their transformation into smart cities. On the other hand, the cities offering good public services, more opportunities for quality jobs, connectivity, and forward-looking environment policies will competitively attract new talents, investments, knowledge, opportunities, and wealth. Particularly in the age of high labor mobility (another driver of change), they will push up the demands for high-quality, lifetime learning, to which, the city management must be responsive. As Seoul in the Republic of Korea has demonstrated—and more recently, Shenzhen in PRC—cities can promote innovation and entrepreneurship in new areas, such as "green" jobs, sustainable transport, and other essential elements for sustainable growth.

Realizing this vision of future education and smart cities cannot be done by one government or one city alone. Smart partnerships and collaboration are prerequisites. In order to avoid costly duplications and to build on emerging innovative good practices, it is important to promote synergies with partners that can bring new ideas, expertise, and financing to work together to scale up good practices in development. Such partnerships can take many forms. One could be, what I call "public–private–people–partnership (PPPP)," bringing together the municipalities' roles and the financing and technical expertise, supported by new technology solutions. Another could be the university-industry linkages to address the skills–job mismatch challenge. I also believe that no initiative can thrive without knowledge partnerships, whatever sector we are talking about (Figure 7.4).

The following speech calls on the youth of ASEAN and Asia to actively shape a brighter future amid the transformative effects of COVID-19. It advocates for technology investment to ensure universal education access and identifies five main drivers of change: economic progress, urbanization, climate change, demographic shifts, and disruptive technology. The speech stresses the importance of acquiring new skills to thrive in the evolving job market. Embracing change and fostering lifelong learning are also encouraged, underscoring the role of youth leadership in tackling global challenges and advancing toward a sustainable future by "building forward better."

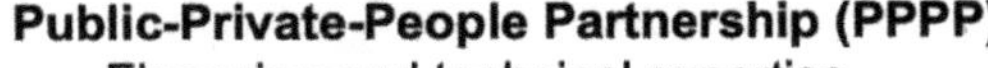

**Public-Private-People Partnership (PPPP)**
- Financing and technical expertise
- Work with municipalities
- EdTech solutions

**University-Industry Linkages**
- Job-ready skills, entrepreneurship and innovation

**Knowledge Partnerships**
- Build on unique expertise

**Figure 7.4** Smart Partnerships and Collaboration
Source: Adapted from ADB (2022b).

## 7.8 Empowering Youth for a Better Future

What I would like to do is to give you an idea of how the youth can get involved in making everyone's lives better—in a way that lasts and gets better even as things change. And, as you know, they change all the time. I don't have to tell you how this COVID-19 pandemic is changing how we do things.

We live in an increasingly volatile, uncertain, complex, and ambiguous (VUCA) world. COVID-19 affected everything—from our health to how we learn, how we work and how we live. It really changed how education works—for different people and across different countries. In countries with good internet access, available computers, laptops, and mobile phones, students have been able to continue learning. It took a while to get it organized. But it is getting easier to handle, and you are all getting better at using these tools.

But in less developed countries, it is not as easy. Students and schools cannot access good, reliable internet connections, or even use computers. We should be worried about that because we can lose a whole generation of smart people who really want to learn. We really need to invest more in the technology that lets everyone get connected to learn—and have fun doing so.

There are many things in daily life which we now can do online. For example, we can hold conferences like this. We can have graduations, doctor consultations, do shopping, banking, order food, and much more. How it expands after the pandemic depends on many things. And that's why it is so important for you, the future generation, to be prepared to adapt to what comes next.

Let me get a bit technical for a moment. Asia is a very different place today than it was a decade ago. There are five main reasons:

(i) The first is economic progress. The Asia region is rapidly working its way out of poverty. In 1981, 1.6 billion people were considered extremely poor. Around 35 years later, we had reduced to about 7% (ADB, 2020c). Before the pandemic hit, the region did well in reducing poverty. But because of COVID-19, about 78 million more people slipped back into extreme poverty (ADB, 2021c). We need to stop the widening inequality between rich and poor in our society. We must ensure everyone benefits from economic recovery.

(ii) Second is our fast-growing cities, or what we call rapid urbanization. Today, more than half of the people in Asia live in cities. By 2050, it could reach two-thirds (ADB, 2019c). People see opportunities in cities—to make a better living for their families. The pandemic could actually accelerate urbanization as people flock to the cities looking for new jobs. So, there will be more and more pressure on cities, on the infrastructure to move people around, and on the social systems that provide quality of life.

(iii) The third reason is climate change. If we don't do something now, it will reverse many of the positive things we have done. I think most of you have seen how climate change impacts weather patterns, worsens typhoons, creates disasters, both droughts and floods, and damages nature, like coral reefs. We must both adapt to and mitigate carbon emissions. Decarbonization may become the mantra for your generation.

(iv)  Then there is demographic change. Some countries in Asia are already aging rapidly, but others still hold a demographic dividend. Countries with relatively young populations must create good jobs and ensure you have the skills to do them. There are also countries with aging populations that need to think about social protection. They need to think about using new technology to produce more with fewer people, increasing labor market efficiency.

(v)  Finally, there is disruptive technology, which basically means out with the old and in with the new. Technology is now the game changer. COVID-19 is accelerating digitalization and the transformation coming from the so-called Fourth Industrial Revolution (IR4.0). The types of skills we will need 10 or 20 years from now will be very different from the ones most people need today. So, we need to prepare. I know most of you will easily learn to use the new technology. How we adapt it to make our lives better is the real challenge.

As I said, with the world becoming more and more digitized, jobs are changing. So, it's not just how we learn. It is what we learn that must also change. The Fourth Industrial Revolution will replace old jobs with new ones. Routine and manual jobs will be the first to disappear. There will be new jobs 10 years from now we can't even imagine today. That's where you come in. These new skills will require what they call STEAM (science, technology, engineering, the arts, and mathematics. Creativity and innovation will be essential. It is your ticket to successfully tap the future job market.

Across the world, old jobs are being replaced by new ones. And entirely new ways of doing business arrive almost daily! Yes, we need to learn. But learning how to learn is perhaps the most important. Sometime in your life you will change positions, and perhaps you may probably change your profession too. That's why you must never stop learning. Lifetime learning will become another mantra.

New professions will emerge. You folks take influencers and YouTubers for granted—just a few years ago my own children would not have believed that could be a career possibility. What's in store? There will be new opportunities in e-commerce, artificial intelligence, data science, data security, robotics, genetics, medicine, and space technology. Don't forget about the arts. For example, Anime transformed animation, which inhabits the virtual world but also influences the real world. Some of my friends' children are your age and earn a lot as content creators. That is just a taste of what's to come.

The world is changing rapidly. And people are also changing. Societies evolve—sometimes too slowly for our liking. But they do. It's really hard to characterize generations. Millennials, as other generations, are a unique bunch. You embrace new technology, adapt it to what you need to do, and make it better. It provides a great opportunity to move things forward, with your feet firmly planted in reality and science, leaving your imagination free to find solutions and answers to the problems and questions we have today.

So it is the youth who must lead our future. Use new technology wisely. As we become better connected, we are better able to learn about and respect all cultures. When we are comfortable with our national pride, we can move on to regional cooperation and regional pride. And then we take a global view—the well-being and coexistence of all people on our planet.

A lot of people say that after the pandemic we need to build back better. I say we need to "build forward better." Our global problems necessitate good solutions. Use your critical thinking to analyze and find better ones. Then put them into practice. Whether for the economy, our society or even in your neighborhood, you will make our earth a better and more livable place.

## 8.1 These Critical Issues Will Define the Future

The previous chapters all define the development trends well in place before the COVID-19 struck. But the pandemic gave them more focus and, in many cases, accelerated progress. The crisis demanded action first on containing the virus and its spread. Emergency support and stimulus financing were then added to keep food on the table for households and essential businesses running. Despite interruptions from new, more virulent variants, recovery plans were already being forged by governments and private businesses. To various degrees—largely dependent on their current state of development and local context—each trend became an important element in recovery plans. The region's vast diversity in social and economic needs between and within countries helped form the

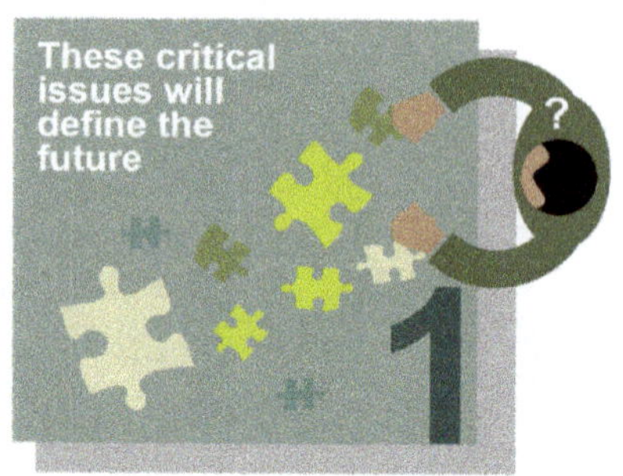


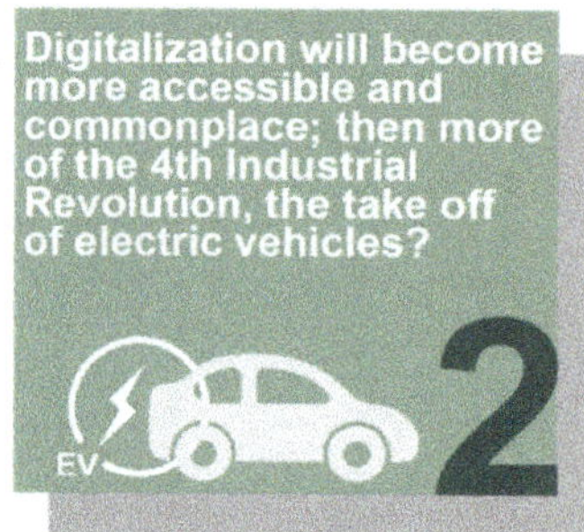

**Figure 8.1** Building Forward Better is the Way Forward

sequence and priorities for initial recovery and longer-term development strategies. All the chapters of this book overlap, as the overriding goal of creating a sustainable, equitable, inclusive, and green future for Asia and the Pacific remains the implicit goal as recovery plans progress. There are many other aspects that will affect the future agenda by region and country—changing demographics, for example. Yet the overall theme for the future of development has changed. It is to build *forward* better, because that *is* the way forward (Figure 8.1).

## 8.2 Digitalization Will Become More Accessible and Commonplace; Then More of the Fourth Industrial Revolution, the Takeoff of Electric Vehicles?

Digitalization is merely the current technological advance spreading rapidly across sectors—just as the internet was in the 1990s and smart phones in the 2000s and just in time efficiency in the 2010s, among others. Innovative technology continues apace. When it allows people to be more productive or communicate better it tends to have a greater impact. What's next? Artificial Intelligence, conquering Big Data, satellite imagery, energy efficiency, and battery technology allowing for the proliferation of electric vehicles; these are the seeds to of new innovation and technology that will continue to shape the development of the Fourth Industrial Revolution and beyond. All these technologies are of course currently available. But their increasingly intensive use and—with digital access growing more inclusive—will dominate the new technology that becomes globally accessible this decade. Building forward will increasingly allow these technologies to work together form greater knowledge and productivity.

## 8.3 Lifelong Learning Yes; But What's Most Valuable?—Productivity vs Wellness

As education and skills development adapt to successive new normals, and new technology, so will the learning process, how it is done—face-to-face and long distance. At 50, people will be re-tuned to start new careers; they will be able to work into their 70s. It is a process that flows from early government systems to private sector-sponsored programs that cross skill levels so as not to force graduates into lifelong commitments to specific firms. Flexibility must be engrained. Yet throughout work–life balances must be kept. Work should not be a burden compared to the rewards accrued—whether in terms of value or personal or familial or community satisfaction.

## 8.4 Climate Impact Likely Greater; "Just Transition" to Accelerate—Maybe Not?

Critical, urgent needs, hard choices, new ways, and attitudes required. From top leaders to local communities. It is happening, so long as people see and read the right stuff. Here demonstrations of projects work wonders. But avoid the demonstration of increasing disasters and suffering. Programs will increasingly be embedded in government plans and development strategies. Cooperation is critical for standards set and timelines sequenced. Communication and awareness of necessary changes will be a central premise.

## 8.5 Climate Finance is Crucial; Availability and Adequacy of Funds Require Innovations

Countries in Asia and Pacific are establishing ambitious targets to tackle climate change. Efforts to foster sustainable development and mitigate the adverse effects of climate change are underway and continually expanding.

Climate finance plays a crucial role in supporting these endeavors. However, ensuring the sustained availability and adequacy of funds necessitates innovation. Strategies and programs to supporting such innovations are also essential to produce more effective and efficient measures, along with collaborations between different stakeholders.

## 8.6 Demand and Profit Will Drive Connectivity; Along with the Need to be Green, Environmentally Sustainable, and Climate Resilient

From food delivery to supply chain logistics, the pandemic brought innovation and new ways of addressing an urgent need for more access to efficient connectivity. Whether for the cross-border movement of goods and services, or better ways of delivering e-commerce purchases, the demand for new, green, more efficient infrastructure is increasingly needed. Costs are well beyond the budgets of most governments, so the private sector must get involved, either through public–private partnerships, government guarantees to reduce risk, bond issuance, or straight private, bankable investments. Infrastructure projects are becoming increasingly complex and use a mixture of these financing modes.

## 8.7 SDGs Pie in the Sky; Each Needs Better Long-Term Sequencing

The 2030 Sustainable Development Goals are a massive global effort to move forward on an ambitious set of social and economic aspirations. From eradicating extreme poverty to quality education for all to gender equity, youth and institutional collaboration, the SDGs, however, finely defined by specific targets and indicators, remain long term, most only attainable well beyond the 2030 deadline. In Asia and the Pacific, none are on track, and the pandemic only delayed many of them further. But they are nonetheless critical to building forward better. Many can be the underlying theme behind recovery and future development plans that are ever more inclusive by involving local communities—and changing mindsets—in the development process. In fact, some aspect of the SDGs is engrained in each of the topics in each of the chapters.

# References

Abbas, S. (2023). Regional assessment of the status of ecosystems as nature-based solutions for climate action: Underscoring the role of blue carbon ecosystems in Asia and the Pacific.

ADB. & ADBI. (2009). Infrastructure for a seamless Asia.

ADB. (2011a). Asia 2050: Realizing the Asian century.

ADB. (2011b). 3 billion Asians could become affluent by 2050—Asia 2050 draft report.

ADB. (2014). Biodiversity landscapes and livelihoods. https://gms-eoc.org/biodiversity-conservation-corridors-initiative

ADB. (2017a). Peshawar sustainable bus rapid transit corridor project.

ADB. (2017b). Meeting Asia's infrastructure needs. Manila.

ADB. (2018). Boosting strategy 2030: Addressing remaining poverty and reducing inequalities. https://www.adb.org/multimedia/donor-report2018/addressing-poverty-reducing-inequalities.html

ADB. (2019a). Cloud-based core banking in the Philippines. Manila.

ADB. (2019b). Strategy 2030 operational plan for priority 3.

ADB. (2019c). Fostering growth and inclusion in Asia's cities.

ADB. (2019d). Strategy 2030 operational plan for priority 4.

ADB. (2020a). Multi-modal transport connectivity for greater sustainability and resiliency.

ADB. (2020b). Asian development outlook 2020 update: Wellness in worrying times.

ADB. (2020c). Asia's journey to prosperity.

ADB. (2021a). Asian economic integration report 2021: Making digital platforms work for Asia and the Pacific. http://dx.doi.org/10.22617/TCS210048-2

ADB. (2021b). Supporting primary health care in Mongolia.

ADB. (2021c). ADB's work on social development and poverty. https://www.adb.org/what-we-do/topics/social-development/overview

ADB. (2021d). From Kyoto to Paris–Transitioning the clean development mechanism.

ADB. (2021e). ADB issues first blue bond for ocean investments. https://www.adb.org/news/adb-issues-first-blue-bond-ocean-investments

ADB. (2021f). Green and resilient rural recovery through agri-food system transformation in the Asia and Pacific region.

ADB. (2021g). ADB, partners to set up new platform to catalyze investments in sustainable infrastructure in Asia. https://www.adb.org/news/adb-partners-new-platform-catalyze-investments-sustainable-infrastructure-asia

ADB. (2021h). Innovative infrastructure financing through value capture in Indonesia.

ADB. (2021i). Asian transport outlook.

ADB. (2021j). COVID-19 and social protection in Asia and the Pacific.

ADB. (2021k). ADB brief: Assessing the impact of the graduation approach in the Philippines.

ADB. (2022a). Building regulatory and supervisory technology ecosystems.

ADB. (2022b). Fintech policy tool kit for regulators and policy makers in Asia and the Pacific.

ADB. (2022c). Strategy 2030 digital technology directional guide: Supporting inclusive digital transformation for Asia and the Pacific.

ADB. (2022d). Strategy 2030 education sector directional guide.

ADB. (2022e). Carbon pricing for energy transition and decarbonization.

ADB. (2022f). Strategy 2030 finance sector directional guide.

ADB. (2022g). Mainstreaming nature-positive investments for green, resilient and inclusive recovery.

ADB. (2022h). Realizing India's potential for transit-oriented development and land value capture.

ADB. (2022i). ACGF overview. https://www.adb.org/what-we-do/funds/asean-catalytic-green-finance-facility/overview

ADB. (2023a). Fiji 2019–2023.

ADB. (2023b). Community resilience partnership program.

ADB. (2023c). Climate change action plan, 2023–2030.

ADB. (2023d). Regional flyway initiative.

ADB. (2023e). Strategy 2030 transport sector directional guide.

ADB. (2023f). Resettling urban populations.

ADB. (2024a). Aging well in Asia.

ADB. (2024b). ADB's work in the energy sector. https://www.adb.org/what-we-do/topics/energy/overview

ADB, UN Women. (2018). Gender equality and the sustainable development goals in Asia and the Pacific: Baseline and pathways for transformative change by 2030.

ADB. (2018). Transport sector study.

Altieri, A. H., & Diaz, R. J. (n.d.). Dead zones: Oxygen depletion in coastal ecosystems. In C. Sheppard (Ed.), World seas: An environmental evaluation.

Andrew, N. L., Bright, P., de la Rua, L., Teoh, S. J., & Vickers, M. (2019). Coastal proximity of populations in 22 Pacific Island Countries and Territories. PLoS One, 14(9), e0223249.

APEC. (2023). Results of the survey for the status of aquaculture in APEC economies.

ASEAN. (2023a). Study on decarbonising the ASEAN agriculture and forestry sector.

ASEAN. (2023b). ASEAN charts course for a sustainable future with ambitious ASEAN strategy for carbon neutrality. https://asean.org/asean-charts-course-for-a-sustainable-future-with-ambitious-asean-strategy-for-carbon-neutrality/

ASEAN. (2023c). RCEP agreement enters into force for Indonesia. https://asean.org/rcep-agreement-enters-into-force-for-indonesia/

Asian Transport Outlook. (2022a). 2021 report on the status of transport-related SDG targets in Asia and the Pacific.

Asian Transport Outlook. (2022b). Asian transport 2030 outlook.

Asian Transport Outlook. (2023). 2023 climate tracker for transport in Asia & Pacific.

Bachas, P., Gertler, P., Higgins, S., & Seira, E. (2018). Digital financial services go a long way: Transaction costs and financial inclusion. American Economic Association Papers and Proceedings, 108, 444–448. https://doi.org/10.1257/pandp.20181013

Bakong. (n.d.). The next-generation mobile payments and banking. https://bakong.nbc.org.kh/en/

BBC. (2021). COP26: India PM Narendra Modi pledges net zero by 2070. https://www.bbc.com/news/world-asia-india-59125143

Bertaud, A. (2015). Cities as labour markets. OECD.

Bloomberg Intelligence. (2024). ESG AUM set to top $40 trillion by 2030, anchor capital markets. https://www.bloomberg.com/professional/insights/sustainable-finance/esg-aum-set-to-top-40-trillion-by-2030-anchor-capital-markets/

Boudreau, D., McDaniel, M., Sprout, E., & Turgeon, A. (2023). Asia: Physical geography. National Geographic. https://education.nationalgeographic.org/resource/asia/

BPS. (2021). The percentage of poor people in September 2020 increased to 10.19 percent. https://www.bps.go.id/en/pressrelease/2021/02/15/1851/the-percentage-of-poor-people-in-september-2020-increased-to-10-19-percent.html

Capgemini Research Institute. (2023). World payments report 2023.

Convention on Biological Diversity. (2022). COP 15: Final text of Kunming-Montreal global biodiversity framework. https://www.cbd.int/article/cop15-final-text-kunming-montreal-gbf-221222

Cambridge Centre for Alternative Finance, ADBI, & FinTechSpace. (2019). ASEAN FinTech ecosystem benchmarking study. https://www.jbs.cam.ac.uk/wp-content/uploads/2020/08/2019-ccaf-asean-fintech-ecosystem-benchmarking-study.pdf. Cambridge, UK.

CDL. (2022). CDL's integrated sustainability report 2022 zeroes in on bolder decarbonization targets. https://www.cdl.com.sg/newsroom/cdls-integrated-sustainability-report-2022-zeroes-in-on-bolder-decarbonisation-targets

Chen, S., Song, Y., & Gao, P. (2023). Environmental, social, and governance (ESG) performance and financial outcomes: Analyzing the impact of ESG on financial performance. Journal of Environmental Management, 345, 118829.

Chetan-Welsh, H., & Hendry, L. (2022). How are climate change and biodiversity loss linked? Natural History Museum. https://www.nhm.ac.uk/discover/how-are-climate-change-and-biodiversity-loss-linked.html

Christie, P. & Ole-Moiyoi, L. K. (2011). Status of marine protected areas and fish refugia in the Bay of Bengal large marine ecosystem.

Clark, J. (2021). Comparison of cost and construction times of first metro lines in Asia. Future Southeast Asia. https://futuresoutheastasia.com/comparison-of-first-metro-lines-in-asia/

Climate Governance Initiative. (2024). Carbon pricing around the world. https://hub.climate-governance.org/resource/carbon-pricing-navigator/carbon-pricing-in-asia-pacific

Center for Strategic and International Studies & McAfee. (2018). Economic impact of cybercrime – No slowing down.

de Sartiges, D., Bharadwaj, A., Khan, I., Tasiaux, J., & Witschi, P. (2020). Southeast Asian consumers are driving a digital payment revolution. Boston Consulting Group. https://image-src.bcg.com/Images/BCG-Southeast-Asian-Consumers-Are-Driving-a-Digital-Payment-Revolution-May-2020_tcm9-247804.pdf

Ellen MacArthur Foundation & UNEP (2023). The global commitment 2023 progress report.

Farooq, S., Naghavi, N., & Scharwatt, C. (2016). Driving a price revolution: Mobile money in international remittances. GSM Association. https://www.gsma.com/mobilefordevelopment/wp-content/uploads/2016/10/2016_GSMA_Driving-a-price-revolution-Mobile-money-in-international-remittances.pdf

Financial Stability Board. (2020). Enhancing cross-border payments: Stage 3 roadmap. https://www.fsb.org/wp-content/uploads/P131020-1.pdf

Firdaus, F. M., Elliot, B., & Ibanez, D. (2023). Southeast Asian cities have some of the most polluted air in the world. World Resources Institute. https://www.wri.org/insights/air-pollution-southeast-asia-cities-jakarta-el-nino

Fujitsu. (2022). How Asia is destined to play a key role in building a more sustainable world.

Italian G20 Presidency. (2021). Third finance ministers and central bank governors meeting.

Ganesha Ecosphere. (2018). About us. https://www.ganeshaecosphere.com/about-us

Garg, A., Kumar, A., & Gupta, N. C. (2021). Comprehensive study on impact assessment of lockdown on overall ambient air quality amid COVID-19 in Delhi and its NCR, India. Journal of Hazardous Materials Letters, 2, 100010.

Gavrilenko. (2020). The K-shaped recovery. https://www.weforum.org/agenda/2020/12/k-shaped-covid19-coronavirus-recovery/

GEF. (2021). Partnerships for coral reef finance and insurance in Asia and the Pacific.

Global Emerging Markets Risk Database. (2024). Global emerging markets: About us. https://www.gemsriskdatabase.org/

Ghahremanloo, M., Lops, Y., Choi, Y., & Mousavinezhad, S. (2021). Impact of the COVID-19 outbreak on air pollution levels in East Asia. Science of the Total Environment, 754, 142226.

Global Taskforce of Local and Regional Governments. (2016). Roadmap for localizing the SDGs. Implementation and monitoring at subnational level.

Government of the Republic of Korea, Financial Services Commission. (2021). FSC grants Toss Bank final approval to operate digital banking business. https://www.fsc.go.kr/eng/pr010101/76052

GSMA. (2012). Mobile money in the Philippines – The market, the models and regulation.

GSMA. (2019). The mobile economy Asia Pacific 2019.

GSMA. (2023). The mobile economy Asia Pacific 2023.

GSMA. (2024). Mobile money metrics database. https://www.gsma.com/mobilemoneymetrics/#global

Globe Telecom Inc. (2021). GCash drives PH digital transformation, hits over PHP 1 trillion transactions in 2020. https://www.globe.com.ph/about-us/newsroom/917ventures/gcash-drives-ph-digital-transformation.html#gref

HELP, Water and Disasters. (2022a). A sustainable ocean economy for 2050: Approximating its benefits and costs.

HELP, Water and Disasters. (2022b). Principles to foster peace before, during, and after water-related hazards.

HSEP. (2022). Overview: Health system enhancement project. https://www.hsep.lk/index.php/who-we-are/about-hsep/overview

Hutton, G. & Varughese, M. (2016). The costs of meeting the 2030 sustainable development goal targets on drinking water, sanitation, and hygiene. World Bank Group.

HELP. (2024a). Vietnam. https://icapcarbonaction.com/en/ets/vietnam

HELP. (2024b). Philippines. https://icapcarbonaction.com/en/ets/philippines

IDMC. (2023). 2023 global report on internal displacement.

IISD. (2020). Japan, Republic of Korea pledge to go carbon-neutral by 2050. https://sdg.iisd.org/news/japan-republic-of-korea-pledge-to-go-carbon-neutral-by-2050/

International Transport Forum. (2020). COVID-19 transport: How badly will the coronavirus crisis hit global freight? https://www.itf-oecd.org/sites/default/files/global-freight-covid-19.pdf

IMF. (2023). Transforming public finance through GovTech.

IPBES. (2018). The regional assessment report on biodiversity and ecosystem services for Asia and the Pacific: Summary for policymakers.

ITU. (2023). Facts and figures 2023. https://www.itu.int/itu-d/reports/statistics/2023/10/10/ff23-youth-internet-use/

IQAir. (2018). 2018 world air quality report.

Abdul Latif Jameel Poverty Action Lab. (2022). Teaching at the right level to improve learning. https://www.povertyactionlab.org/case-study/teaching-right-level-improve-learning

JICA. (2018). Feasibility study on The North South Railway Project – South Line (Commuter) (North-South Commuter Railway Extension Project) in the Republic of the Philippines.

Juneja, M., De Souza, C., Giriyan, A. L., & Ganeshan, S. (2021). Contextualising blue economy in Asia-Pacific region. The Energy and Resources Institute.

Larsen, G., & Laxton, V. (2024). Development banks are starting to spark climate action. Will they complete the task? World Resources Institute. https://www.wri.org/insights/mdb-reform-climate-action

Mapa, D. S. (2020). Damages due to natural extreme events and disasters amounted to PhP 463 billion. Philippine Statistics Authority. https://psa.gov.ph/content/damages-due-natural-extreme-events-and-disasters-amounted-php-463-billion

Marcus, J. (2018). Saving mangroves: A new worldwide partnership aims to protect and restore a critical ecosystem. World Wildlife Fund. https://www.worldwildlife.org/magazine/issues/summer-2018/articles/saving-mangroves

Marriott, P., & Aggarwal, N. (2023). Why the battle for net-zero may be won or lost by corporate Asia. World Economic Forum. https://www.weforum.org/agenda/2023/04/how-corporate-asia-sits-at-the-centre-of-the-climate-crisis-but-also-its-solution/

Multilateral Development Banks and IMF (2020). Financing the sustainable development goals.

McGrath, M. (2020). Climate change: China aims for 'carbon neutrality by 2060'. BBC News. https://www.bbc.com/news/science-environment-54256826

Nedopil, C., Larsen, M., Chane-Yook, A., & Narain, D. (2024). Catching up with climate priorities: Understanding multilateral development banks' evolving approach to biodiversity. Global Policy.

OECD, WTD, IMF (2020). Handbook on measuring digital trade.

OECD & UCLG (2019). 2019 report of the world observatory on subnational government finance and investment. Paris/Barcelona.

Oregon State University. (2018). International river basins in Asia. https://transboundarywaters.ceoas.oregonstate.edu/gallery-image/international-river-basins-asia-2018

Oxford Insights. (2023). Government AI readiness index.

Parada, J., & Pirlea, F. (2023). Ending overfishing: An urgent need to protect our oceans. World Bank Blogs. https://blogs.worldbank.org/en/opendata/ending-overfishing-urgent-need-protect-our-oceans

PayNet. (2017). Regional collaboration for real-time cross-border payments across Asia [Press release].

Penuel, W. R., Briggs, D. C., Davidson, K. L., Herlihy, C., Sherer, D., Hill, H. C., Farrell, C., & Allen, A. (2017). How school and district leaders access, perceive, and use research. AERA Open, 3(2).

PLN. (2022). Consolidated ESG performance report 2022.

Prud'homme, R., & Lee, C. W. (1999). Size, sprawl, speed and the efficiency of cities. Urban Studies, 36(11), 1849-1858.

Railway Technology. (2024). North-South Railway Project, Philippines. https://www.railway-technology.com/projects/north-south-railway-project/?cf-view

Rakhiemah, A. N., Zharifah, N., Shidiq, M., Pradnyaswari, I., Rizaldi, M. I., & Suryadi, B. (2024). Progress of carbon pricing in ASEAN to support the shift toward a low carbon economy.

Regan. (2024). The world's 100 worst polluted cities are in Asia – and 83 of them are in just one country. CNN. https://edition.cnn.com/2024/03/18/climate/air-pollution-report-2023-asia-climate-intl-hnk/index.html

Rapsomanikis, G. (2015). The economic lives of smallholder farmers. Food and Agriculture Organization.

Republic of Indonesia. (2022). Enhanced nationally determined contribution Republic of Indonesia.

Sachs, J., Schmidt-Traub, G., Kroll, C., Lafortune, G., & Fuller, G. (2019). Sustainable development report 2019. Bertelsmann Stiftung and Sustainable Development Solutions Network.

South Asia Subregional Economic Cooperation. (2017). Trade facilitation. https://www.sasec.asia/index.php?page=trade-facilitation

Sharif, M. M. (2023). It's all about cities: We mustn't flip the coin on sustainable investment.

SOURCE. (2020). SOURCE highlighted for 'systemic' potential by the G20 finance ministers and central bank governors. https://public.sif-source.org/sif-source-news/source-highlighted-for-systemic-potential-by-the-g20-finance-ministers-and-central-bank-governors/

SWIFT. (2019). Taking the pulse of ISO 20022 adoption by APAC securities market infrastructures [Swift Info Paper].

*Statista.* (2024a). Retail e-commerce market volume worldwide in 2023, by region. https://www.statista.com/statistics/311357/sales-of-e-commerce-worldwide-by-region/

*Statista.* (2024b). Internet usage in the Asia-Pacific region – statistics & facts. https://www.statista.com/topics/9080/internet-usage-in-the-asia-pacific-region/#topicOverview

*Statista.* (2024c). Value of green bonds issued worldwide from 2014 to 2023, by region. https://www.statista.com/statistics/1294449/value-of-green-bonds-issued-worldwide-by-region/

TEEB. (2010). Mainstreaming the economics of nature. TEEB Geneva.

Tonik. (2021). Tonik launches as first neobank in the Philippines [News release].

Transboundary Freshwater Diplomacy Database, College of Earth, Ocean, and Atmospheric Sciences, Oregon State University. (2018). International river basins of Asia. https://transboundarywaters.ceoas.oregonstate.edu/gallery-image/international-river-basins-asia-2018

UCLG. (2019a). The localization of the global agendas. How local action is transforming territories and communities (Asia-Pacific Region). Barcelona.

UCLG. (2019b). The localization of the global agendas. How local action is transforming territories and communities. Barcelona.

UK Government. (n.d.). Global Ocean Alliance. https://www.gov.uk/government/topical-events/global-ocean-alliance-30by30-initiative/about#global-ocean-alliance-members

UN. (2020). Decade of action. https://www.un.org/sustainabledevelopment/decade-of-action/

UN. (2021). Trade facilitation in times of crisis and pandemic. Practices and lessons from the Asia-Pacific region.

UN. (2024). 2024 theme: MSMEs and the SDGs. https://www.un.org/en/observances/micro-small-medium-businesses-day

UN, ADB, & UNDP. (2022). Building forward together: Towards an inclusive and resilient Asia and the Pacific.

UNCTAD. (2014). World investment report 2014: Investing in the SDGs: An action plan.

UNDP (Regional Hub for Asia-Pacific). (2021). SDG localization in Asia and the Pacific [Programming Note]. Bangkok.

UNEP (2017). Building resilience to disasters and conflicts. https://www.unep.org/regions/asia-and-pacific/regional-initiatives/building-resilience-disasters-and-conflicts

UNEP. (2021). Adaptation gap report 2021.

UNEP. (2023). Nations must go further than current Paris pledges or face global warming of 2.5-2.9°C. https://www.unep.org/news-and-stories/press-release/nations-must-go-further-current-paris-pledges-or-face-global-warming

UNESCAP. (2024). Asia and the Pacific SDG progress report 2024.

United Nations Educational, Scientific and Cultural Organization. (2024). World education statistics.

UNESCO Institute of Statistics. (2024). Gross enrolment ratio in tertiary education. https://ourworldindata.org/grapher/gross-enrollment-ratio-in-tertiary-education

UNHCR. (2020). Global trends: Forced displacement in 2020.

UNICEF. (2021). Most countries in Asia-Pacific off-track to achieve SDG4 targets despite increasing numbers of children going to school. https://www.unicef.org/rosa/press-releases/most-countries-asia-pacific-track-achieve-sdg4-targets-despite-increasing-numbers

UOB, PwC, & SFA. (2020). FinTech in ASEAN 2020: Get up, reset, go! https://www.uobgroup.com/techecosystem/news-insights-fintech-in-asean-2020.html#funding

UOB, PwC, & SFA. (2022). FinTech in ASEAN 2022: Finance, reimagined. https://www.uobgroup.com/techecosystem/news-insights-fintech-in-asean-2022.html

Vivid Economics. (2021). Greenness of stimulus index.

We Are Social. (2018, January 30). Digital in 2018: World's internet users pass the 4 billion mark. We Are Social USA. https://wearesocial.com/us/blog/2018/01/global-digital-report-2018/

Wetzel, C. (2021). The planet has lost half of its coral reefs since 1950. Smithsonian Magazine. https://www.smithsonianmag.com/science-nature/the-planet-has-lost-half-of-coral-reefs-since-1950-180978701/

WHO. (2018). COP24 special report: Health & climate change.

WHO. (2023). Global status report on road safety 2023.

Woetzel, J., Krishnan, M., Madgavkar, A., Ellingrud, K., Yee, L., Gupta, R., Seong, J., & Devillard, S. (2018). The power of parity: Advancing women's equality in Asia Pacific. McKinsey & Company.

World Bank. (2018). World development report.

World Bank. (2020). Global financial inclusion (Global Findex) database and world development indicators. Washington, DC.

World Bank. (2023a). Striving for clean air: Air pollution and public health in South Asia.

World Bank. (2023b). Total fisheries production (metric tons). https://data.worldbank.org/indicator/ER.FSH.PROD.MT?end=2022&most_recent_value_desc=true&start=1960&view=chart&year_high_desc=true

World Bank. (2023c). State and trends of carbon pricing.

World Bank. (2024a). School enrollment, tertiary (% gross). https://genderdata.worldbank.org/en/indicator/se-ter-enrr?view=trend&geos=IDN_MYS_THA_PHL&gender=female

World Bank. (2024b). Global carbon pricing revenues top a record $100 billion.

World Economic Forum. (2024). Global risks report 2024.

WTO. (2020). Trade shows signs of rebound from COVID-19, recovery still uncertain. https://www.wto.org/english/news_e/pres20_e/pr862_e.htm

Zetter, K. (2016, May 17). That insane, $81M Bangladesh bank heist? Here's what we know. WIRED. https://www.wired.com/2016/05/insane-81m-bangladesh-bank-heist-heres-know/

Zhang, Z. (2021). China's digital yuan: Development status and possible impact for businesses. China Briefing.

# Index